COAL CAMP KIDS

GROWING UP IN A COAL CAMP

Margie J Pittman

authorHOUSE®

AuthorHouse™
1663 Liberty Drive
Bloomington, IN 47403
www.authorhouse.com
Phone: 1-800-839-8640

First published by AuthorHouse 5/2/2011

ISBN: 978-1-4567-6773-0 (sc)
ISBN: 978-1-4567-6772-3 (dj)
ISBN: 978-1-4567-6771-6 (e)

Library of Congress Control Number: 2011906733

Printed in the United States of America

In memory of my sister, Judy Pittman Quentrill.

Dedicated to my four brothers: Larry, Roy, Raymond, and David Pittman, and coal camp kids everywhere.

FORWARD

The stories in this book are true to the extent that memory will allow. Some have been embellished ever so slightly, by time and retelling, as stories often are. Most of the people mentioned in this book have agreed to have their stories told. Some of them even told on themselves, and supplied the stories. A few names have been left out to protect those who may not want their identity revealed. Writing this book was a joy.

You will no doubt realize that proper English is not always used. Despite the valiant efforts of the editors, I felt that the way we spoke at the time better revealed the flavor of the time and place represented. Remembering childhood friends and family is a lot of fun. You don't have to be a coal camp kid to enjoy that. I hope that the final result is that the reader gets a taste of what it was like to be a coal camp kid in days gone by.

INTRODUCTION

"Flies in the buttermilk, shoo, fly, shoo. Flies in the buttermilk, shoo, fly, shoo. Flies in the buttermilk, shoo, fly, shoo. Skip to my Lou, my darling." It was not unusual to hear children singing when you lived in a coal camp. You see, we had to create our own fun. Most of the time, we were quite entertaining. See I'm a coal camp kid. There were quite a few of us growing up in the hills of West Virginia. We went to school, and attended church. We obeyed our parents or suffered the consequences. Since I'm writing this in the age of political correctness, you may not realize that there was a time when you were not only allowed to spank your kids, you were expected to. For the kids I grew up with, climbing the hills and swimming in the creek were great fun. I'm about to tell their story, as well as my own. These are some of the memories that have been taken away from our years growing up in a coal camp during the forties and fifties. So, let's take a walk down memory lane.

Chapter One

WORKING IN THE COAL MINES

Every time I hear Loretta Lynn sing "Coal Miner's Daughter," I can relate to every word she is singing. I know that girls young and old all over West Virginia, and many other states, can relate to the song as well. You see, our daddy's, along with thousands of others, worked in the coal mines. In the early years of my life, Daddy worked for the "Dixport Coal Company." He worked in the Cinco mines, so that is where we lived. It was required. "Cinco, pronounced sin-co," is located on Campbells Creek, right outside of Charleston. Charleston is the capital city of West Virginia. We still refer to ourselves as "Creekers".

From Reed to Putney and everywhere in between, the little communities along Campbells Creek had coal mines. The mines could be a very dangerous place to work. Daddy worked in some deplorable conditions in the Cinco mines. Sometimes he would crawl around on his belly digging that coal out for the company. At times, it was only eighteen inches from the ceiling to the floor of the mines.

The only light they had came from a carbide light they wore on their hard shell hats. I can still remember Daddy's knees swelling up. They would be double their normal size. He told me once he had water on his knees. They were always puffy and red. He would have to go to the doctor to have them treated.

My dad did not live a long life. He died at fifty-four of a heart attack. One time he was almost killed when he got into electricity. One of the other miners saw what happened and ran and pulled the power switch. If he hadn't acted so quickly dad would have died that day. Water often seeped into the mines where my dad worked. It was wet much of the time. Most days, he had to work in the water. Needless to say, it was not a union mine. In spite of the danger and the deplorable conditions, he loved the mines. Most of the guys who worked in the mines, didn't want to work anywhere else.

The work in the mines was hard, and the pay wasn't very good. He would come home as black as the coal he had dug out of the ground. Still he went into the mines each day to make a living for his family. Coal dust was a natural part of our lives. We lived in a company house. As I said earlier, it was a requirement; you had to live in a company house if you wanted to work in their mines. Those were the company rules. You paid them to live in their houses, and you bought everything you used from their company store. They even allowed you to buy on credit. Daddy had a bill at the company store, and I would go in and get a nickel's worth of penny candy and nonchalantly say, "Put it on the bill." I felt special when I did that, like I was from a rich family.

We paid our utilities to the company. We heated and cooked with coal, we had one water pump the whole community used for drinking, cooking, and everything else. By the time they took all of their money out of the worker's checks, there was not much, if anything, left over. Before most weeks were over, the miners were reduced to borrowing "scrip" in order to last them until payday again. That way, the company got most of the money right back. So, actually, it seemed that the miners were working for nothing. The company store got a large portion of the workers' money because they could buy everything they needed there. Of course, they were charged a big price for everything they bought. Most of the men didn't have cars. Daddy finally got one when I was in the fifth grade.

I remember when we first heard the song "Sixteen Ton" by Tennessee Ernie Ford: "You load sixteen ton, and what do you get? Another day older and deeper in debt. St. Peter don't you call me 'cause I can't go. I owe my soul to the company store." There was one line in that song that was offensive to my dad and others: "A mind that's weak and a back that's strong." Coal miners will let you know real fast that there is nothing weak about their minds. Now some miners are not well educated, but it might surprise you to know that some are very educated. Daddy worked with a man who was going to law school while working in the mines. He later became an esteemed judge. We were all very proud of his accomplishments. When one miner succeeded, we could all be happy. We took our victories wherever we found them.

One of my earliest memories was first grade. You see it was a waste of my time. My brother Larry was four years older than me. The year before I started school, Larry would make me play school with him. He was the teacher and I was the student. If I didn't learn something in a timely manner, he would get a switch and threaten me with it. I guess it all worked out for my good; I could count to one hundred, recite my alphabet, and read a first-grade reader all the way through before I had been to school the first day. On the negative side, I hated school for a long time. I related it to "mean old" Larry. As I got older, I realized he was just trying to give me a good start in school. That was the only way he knew how. Mom told me many times how Larry loved his little sister so much that when I was a few weeks old he tried to share his chocolate cake with me. Mom said he had my mouth stuffed full. She had to dig it out so I could breathe. It's a wonder I didn't choke to death on his goodness.

It was funny watching all us girls go to school on the first day in our new dresses. We all dressed alike because that was the only pattern they had at the company store. Sometimes, not often, you could get a different color. We didn't think it odd that every girl in the classroom had on the same dress. It seemed like we had a dress code. Whatever the company store had to sell, that was our dress code. The boys all wore jeans and had similar shirts as well; they were usually plaid. We were coal camp kids, and that's just the way it was.

We all had lots of friends because every woman and man who lived in the camp had a house full of kids. There were at least six or seven per family. We all had the same things; we bought whatever the store provided. We didn't have much choice. Now you might think we had a bad life. I know it sounds that way, but we didn't. For the most part, we were happy kids.

If there was one thing that irked us girls, it was our little brothers. We all had at least two. I had three younger brothers and one older brother. They tattled on us for everything we did. They were always getting us into trouble. All of the mothers in that camp had a switch lying around somewhere. They usually cut a new one every morning. That was just part of their daily routine. If that one broke, they would send you to get your own. How dumb did they think we were? If I knew that the switch I was getting would be used on me of course I got the flimsiest one I could find. However, if I thought that it was for my brothers, I got the biggest one I could find. As it turned out, I usually got it before they did. You see, you couldn't win in the coal camp. We sure tried, though.

I still remember Daddy's dinner bucket. It was round and tall. He carried water in the bottom of the bucket, and his sandwiches fit on the top in another compartment. Daddy always took four sandwiches and a cake or pie to work. Every evening we would run to meet Daddy and get his dinner bucket. He always left something in it for us. We used to fight over it until Mom made us take turns. It was a real treat if daddy left a cake for us to find, but we would eat a sandwich or a half a sandwich if that's what he left. I don't know why it tasted so good after it sat in his lunch bucket all day, but it did. He always made sure there was something left for us.

On a cold winter night, we would all gather around the fire, and Dad would tell us scary stories. The ones we liked the best were "gotcha" stories; you know, the ones that had a scary ending. When everything was really quiet, you waited in anticipation, not knowing when it would happen. All of a sudden, Dad would jump and say, "Gotcha." We knew it was going to end that way. We had heard most of the stories dozens of times, but they always scared us.

In the summertime, us kids would play hide-and-seek, red rover, and tag. We didn't have a lot of toys or games, so we had to find ways of entertaining ourselves, and we did. Sometimes Dad would get out the guitar, and he and I would play and sing with my little sister Judy while sitting on the front porch. Many times Mom would stand in the doorway and sing along. I miss Mom and Dad. They were good parents. Many times our neighbors would stop by and join us. My uncle Sidney would bring over his harmonica, and we'd play and sing until the moon was high in the sky. Before we quit, Daddy would say, "Now let's sing Mommy's, (my grandmother's,) favorite song." We would sing "Jesus Savior, Pilot Me." We always ended the night that way.

Chapter Two

CHURCHGOERS AND SINNERS

In our coal camp, we had two classes of people; there were the churchgoers and the sinners. Well I was a churchgoer. I went to the Baptist church on Sunday morning and the Holiness church on Sunday afternoon. All of us kids did that. One reason we went to the Holiness church was that they gave the kids a candy bar. Times were not like they are today. We could have been bribed with a piece of bubble gum, but candy bars were very hard to come by. I never missed a Sunday. Somehow, even in our meanness, a little seed of faith in Jesus would get through. I was really a Baptist 'cause that's what Daddy was. He used to say, "Girl, you are going to be so confused, you won't know what we are." He only set his foot down one time about going to church. That was the day I climbed on a church bus and rode to Charleston to go to the Pentecostal church. Now that is where he drew the line. Daddy said I would get confused going to so many different churches. I told him they had the best music of any church I had ever been to. He wasn't impressed when I said they had a piano, drums, guitars, and a banjo. Now Daddy loved all those instruments, but like a lot of Baptists back in the day, he thought the church only needed a piano. Well that was one time my beloved father and I disagreed. I loved that music. It spoke to me then, and it still does.

Did I tell you we had a beer joint at the coal camp? Well, actually, it was on the outskirts. Now only the sinners went to the beer joint; we called them bad sinners, and they called us hypocrites. The only time any of us churchgoers went near the beer joint was when the company store was closed and we just had to have a Pepsi-Cola. We would go to the door and someone would bring our pop to us. I never went inside. I don't think that qualifies us as bad sinners. Anyway, half the miners went to the beer joint on Saturday night and half went to church on Sunday morning. They all got along, though, because they had to work together. The mines could be very dangerous. If a sinner got hurt, he needed the Christians to pray for him. It was strange, but somehow it worked. I always knew I was on the winning side; there was only one beer joint, and we had two churches.

One of the best things about our company store was that it had a movie theater in the basement. We never missed a movie. It only cost a dime for kids, and we all went. I still remember those grainy pictures we watched. Most of them were westerns, but we could tolerate that, because in the beginning, they would show a cartoon. That was worth the dime all by itself. My aunt Thelma always went with us. She would make a big bag of popcorn and some potato candy. We had just as much fun as the kids who lived downtown. I guess that by today's standards, we were as poor as church mice. However we didn't know we were poor. You see, we had each other, our parents, the company store with a movie theater, a post office, two churches, a beer joint, and a two-room schoolhouse; we had something for everyone. What more did we need?

I remember when the church had a hot dog dinner. Now all us kids loved hot dogs. It was a treat we didn't get very often. Midgie

Davis was a woman who fell into the sinner category. She told me she was going to donate the chili for the hot dogs. She said she would make all them Baptists drunk, 'cause she made her chili with beer. She said it was the best chili you'd ever eat. I knew I wouldn't touch that chili. Now I loved chili on hot dogs, but I decided not to eat any that night. I knew if I was impaired, I wouldn't be able to watch all night to see if anyone got drunk on her chili. Well, of course, no one did. I just missed a good hot dog with the best chili that most had ever eaten. Now, that was a sin!

I learned years later that even if Midgie Davis had put beer in the chili, the cooking process would have boiled the alcohol out of it. I was only a child, and we didn't have beer at our house. If we did, I didn't know about it. My uncle Sidney did make some home brew once, and Dad tasted a little of that. They hid it from Mom and Aunt Thelma. That worked until my cousins, Linda and her little brother Richard, found the stuff. They got into it and drank until they were so drunk that they couldn't stand up. They were only about four and six at the time. Thelma found them passed out asleep behind the pot belly stove with their cup still in tow. My uncle Sidney almost had to find himself a new home when my aunt Thelma found out what was wrong with them. Of course, my mother got into the act also. She told my daddy he had better never bring any of that slop into her house. She was practicing self-righteous indignation. Daddy never made any home brew after that; Sidney didn't either. If they did they kept it well hid. I never got to taste it. Linda told me that the first drink was awful but it got better with each drink. I felt like I had missed out on something special. That didn't happen very often; I was usually on top of everything.

One of mine and Linda's favorite things to do was rock in the rocking chair and sing to the radio. We would sing as loud as we could. "I'm a Lonely Little Petunia in an Onion Patch" was one of our favorites. It was the forties, and that was a popular song in that day. We would learn the songs from the radio, and then I could play them on the guitar and we could sing them anytime we wanted to.

Chapter Three

A BORN ACTRESS AND HER FAMILY AND FRIENDS

I remember when I had the lead role in our Christmas play at church. Now I gave it all I had. The church was full, and as nervous as I was, I knew I needed to do a good job. I played the part of the rich woman who didn't want to take in her sister's orphaned children. Needless to say, it started off with me being very mean; as a matter of fact, I pounded my fist on the table and complained so loud about the cost of celery, it nearly scared Mary O'Dell to death. Mary was playing the part of my maid, and she was so shocked that she jumped back. I even surprised myself, but I had to make it real; I was an actor. The play ended with me being very repentant. I was sorry for my stingy actions, and I embraced my sister's children. When that play was over, I was exhilarated. I was a born actress. That feeling must have lasted at least three days. I knew I was the star of that play. Midgie Davis told me so the next day; she said she didn't know I could act like that. I remember wondering if I should venture to Hollywood when I got older. Of course, that dream soon died out. Still, it was fun while it lasted.

Now I would like to get back to brothers. I had three younger than me and one older. There was Larry, the oldest and most sophisticated; Roy,who was the meanest; Raymond, who was the most dangerous; and David, the baby, who was the sweetest. I also had a sister; only one, and sometimes she was a disappointment. I loved her more than anything in my world, but she was really girly; you know she played with dolls, dishes, and all that girly stuff. If my brothers got near her, she would scream at them. I can still hear her say, "Get out of here and leave me alone. Then in her loudest shrillest voice she would scream for Mommy. I was a little over five years old when Judy was born, and I had had to play and fight with three brothers up to that point. Even the girls I played with didn't like dolls. We played ball, and us girls beat the boys real good every now and then. However, even Judy did draw the line at some girly things; she hated wearing panties more than anything. I remember Mommy getting her dressed every morning in a clean dress and clean panties. Well, little sister would go out to play, pee in her panties, and throw them in the creek. She would say, "I am not wearing these old stinkies." That was her name for wet panties. Then she would run around with her fanny shining until we caught her. Every week, Mom had to climb on the town bus and go to the five-and-dime store to get Judy some new panties. They had ten pair for a dollar. My sister threw more panties in the creek than I ever had in a lifetime. It got to the point that my mother finally lost her patience and spanked her bare bottom a few times, and then she learned to tolerate panties a little better.

Did I tell you that our creek was one of the places we could all have fun? When it came up a good hard rain, we could dam it up and swim in it. The only problem was that the road went through the creek. When we dammed it up, Joe Waughs couldn't take his horse and sled through it. The creek had other uses for a coal camp kid too. You could get rid of most anything by throwing it in the creek. I remember the old cat that showed up at our house one day. She was pregnant and Mom threw a fit when she had five little kittens. She didn't hurt the cat, but she threatened every day to get rid of those kittens. She would say, "I'd like to take all those doggone old kittens down to the creek and drown them." One evening Mom and Dad went to the store to get our weekly supply of groceries. I was left in charge of the kids. I went looking for Raymond because he had slipped from my view. I found him all right. He was at the creek with a hoe in his hand, holding a little kitten under the water. I screamed at him, "What are you doing?"

He said, "I'm drowning these doggone old kittens for Mommy."

I took the hoe out of his hands and explained that Mommy didn't really mean it; she was just frustrated. Mom had a sheepish look on her face when I told her what Raymond had been doing and what he had said. Dad stepped in and told her she had to be careful what she said in front of us kids. We didn't know when she wasn't really serious. Raymond stayed clear of her for a few days until it all blew over just as it always did in the coal camp. We went on to better things.

Raymond by himself was a little timid. However when you mixed him with his best friends George Hess, Jerry Bartley, and Jerry Dixon, he was as bold as they were. When you mixed in Brother Roy, then you had the equivalent of an atomic bomb.

Like the day our neighbor (I'll call him Mr. M.) had collected him some dark glass bottles. You see he could sell them and make a nice profit. Raymond and Roy had seen them being delivered. There was about three dump-truck loads of glass piled up next to the creek. It stood about eight feet tall. The boys all got together one afternoon to play; somebody picked up a small pebble and threw it at the glass, and it just bounced off. Then they tried again and again, and it bounced off. Then one of the boys picked up a bigger rock, and this time it didn't bounce. It made a loud crash. Nothing pleases a little boy like a loud, destructive crash. Well, the fun was on, and they all lost control.

They threw rocks until the glass was flying everywhere. They gathered up a bucket of rocks to throw. They tried to see who could break two bottles with one rock. When they were through, the eight feet of glass was level with the ground. My daddy came out of the house to work in his garden. When he heard the glass breaking, he knew that Roy and Raymond were involved. He took off to stop the boys and pay Mr. M. for the glass they had broken. They would get a good whipping for that. Just before Dad reached them, Mr. M. went after them. He was cussing and threatening the boys when Daddy walked up on them. He heard him calling them little SOBs. Now, my dad didn't allow us to cuss, and he sure wouldn't stand for someone cussing at us; this was especially true if they were his age. Momentarily, Dad forgot all about what the boys had done. All he heard was a grown man cussing at his family. Now he didn't cuss at his kids and nobody else was going to either. Daddy turned and went after Mr. M. In the words of Raymond, our peace-loving dad slapped the man's smile clear down in his socks. The old man ran into the house, and Dad took the boys home. Of course, the boys were still in some trouble, but after the cussing they had just taken, Daddy figured that was punishment enough. He would see to it that they paid for the glass.

Another day, the same group of little hoodlums went to play on the gob dump. (For those of you who don't know, gob is the waste from the mines, a mixture of dirt and low-grade coal.) To their delight someone had been working there and left their bulldozer. Well, that was an awful lot of temptation for these boys to overcome. Soon they were crawling all over it. Raymond found a button and pushed it, and the engine acted like it was going to start. He moved some levers and knobs around and tried again, and this time the engine started. The bulldozer started moving very slowly. Now the boys didn't know how to turn it off, and they couldn't steer it, so they decided to abandon ship. The big piece of equipment inched its way across the gob dump with all five little boys running along beside it. It didn't stop until it ran into a big tree, and there it sat idling until the men got back. The boys were long gone. They meant no harm; it's just the nature of boys to get into some mischief. They hoped the owner would take that into consideration.

If you have never seen a gob dump, some of them are huge. You could actually walk to the top and slide down the dump, and that was more fun than a seesaw. One day our gob dump started smoking real bad. Everyone said it was burning deep inside. I tell you, I thought my mother was right; she said, "Hell had started in Cinco." It was a little scary, but as kids, our curiosity got the best of us. We went ahead and slid down the gob dump anyway. It was always real warm after that.

There was also a day when Raymond and George Hess started a new fad. They would push their lips out as far as they could, and try to look like they had duck lips. Soon, all their friends picked up the habit. All the little boys in the coal camp were trying to look and talk like ducks. It was Raymond and George's idea, and they were right proud of it. Every time someone tried to talk to them, they would stick out their lips and quack back an answer. I used to tell Mom to make Raymond stop doing that. She would just laugh and say, "Now, he's not hurting you one bit. Just don't look at him." (Can you believe that response?) I just hoped they would freeze like that. I guess that would teach them a lesson. They were just coal camp kids trying to have fun.

One day the boys gathered up a bunch of bicycle tires and rims. They soon realized the tires were not any good. Dad picked up one of the rims, tossed it, and when it landed, it rolled across the yard. Then the boys got the idea to take off the tires and play with the rims. They would take a stick and roll the rims all over the camp. Raymond got so good at it that he could roll his up and down the steps. They thought it was their own invention. It was like a new sport; it occupied them for months.

I'll never forget the summer that Betsy Ferguson came to stay with her sister Aileen. Betsy was raised in poorer conditions than we were. She brought a whole new culture of meanness with her.

She knew things I had never even heard of. She could cuss as well as any man I ever knew. That almost made her a hero in my eyes. Betsy could chew some tobacco now, and she made it look like so much fun that I had to try it. One day we took our tobacco over to the big creek. Not the creek that flowed by our house; this creek was deeper and wider. It was part of Campbells Creek, where we lived. As we sat on the creek bank chewing our tobacco, we came up with a game to play. We wanted to see who could spit the farthest out into the creek. As we sat there chewing and spitting, I guess I let down my guard, 'cause the next thing I heard over Betsy's laughter was the voice of Roy saying, "I'm going to tell Mommy on you for chewing tobacco. That is dirty and nasty." Well, I couldn't chance letting him tell on me, so I did what every self-respecting criminal would do; I tried to bribe him. I offered him a chew. At first, he said no, until Betsy and I showed him just how much fun it was to chew tobacco and spit in the creek. We really put it on thick. I knew if that didn't work, I would be going after the switch that day. Finally, he gave in. See Roy was inquisitive about everything; he just had to try it. So we gave him a big chew, and he chewed it up real good. Then he promptly swallowed it. I knew right then I was in a world of trouble.

We practically carried Roy home and made him swear he would not tell on us. We convinced him he would be in as much trouble as we would be. By the time we got him home, he was so sick that he couldn't walk. His face was as white as new-fallen snow. He laid on the ground moaning until Dad and Mom heard him and came to see what was wrong. He just kept saying, "I am so sick. I'm dying." Roy could not stand up, and being it was the fifties, Mommy thought he had "the polio." (Polio was a bad disease that crippled people suddenly without warning, and there was no way to prevent it back then.) Roy was moaning and Mom was wringing her hands and crying. I was in shock. Still I might have gotten away with it if Mom had not told my dad to go get the company doctor because Roy had the polio for sure.

It was at that point that I saw my life passing before my eyes. I knew I was dead. I spoke up in a trembling voice and confessed what "he" had done. Mom asked where on earth did he get chewing tobacco. It was getting harder all the time to answer her questions. I told her I had given it to him. She said, "Just where did you get chewing tobacco?" I was really in trouble then because Betsy and I had stolen that tobacco out of our houses. The miners, who smoked, chewed tobacco in the mines. (Methane gas made fire of any kind deadly in the mines.) Daddy smoked, so I had sneaked some of his chewing tobacco out of his dinner bucket.

I saw Mom's face go from bright red to dark purple. She was so angry she could have strung me up, and I knew it. Thank God for my daddy; he saved my life. He looked at Mom's angry face, and then at the terror on mine, and he actually got tickled; he wouldn't let Mom kill me. She was so mad that I did get grounded for nearly the rest of my life, it seemed. I think it was actually about a week. It was a long week, though. I couldn't leave the yard. I had to watch all the other kids play and have fun, and I couldn't play with them. "Absolutely no Betsy," that was at the top of Mommy's list. All this drama and no one got into trouble but me. Betsy's sister never knew anything about it. Soon she was out playing with her new friends. One day she stopped by the gate where I was standing all alone and assured me that it was only temporary until I was let out of jail.

Mom said Roy was punished enough by being so sick. After she made him drink soda water and puke up the tobacco, he was okay, but he milked it for all it was worth. To make matters worse, I had to look at the disappointed face of my mother every day, and that was the worst punishment of all. Roy told me after it was over that he sure didn't tell on me. That was like a badge of honor to him. In all his suffering, he had kept his mouth shut for once. I told him I was proud of him for not telling, but I could still wring his little neck for swallowing that tobacco. He could always get me in more trouble than I could ever get out of. I sat down one day and counted up all the sins I had committed on that one little escapade. I had stolen the tobacco, chewed tobacco, lied through my teeth over and over, and almost killed my brother. That week I spent in captivity didn't teach me a thing. Given the chance, I would have done it all over again, with one small exception: I'd go ahead and kill Roy.

Chapter Four

TATTLING ON ROY, PAULINE, LARRY, AND DOG BITING

To this day, I sometimes have the feeling that little brothers are the enemy. One day as I was walking up the road with my friends, we happened to meet up with Roy. Now he could be mean at times, yet he was the sweetest brother in the world at other times. If you have a brother, you know how much you thrive on telling Mommy on each other. It delighted me to get something good on Roy, and he loved getting something on me. Well, I knew I had the ultimate good thing the day Roy cussed out the dog.

The story goes like this. Roy was tagging along that day with me and my friends. I told him to get on up the road, and leave us alone. I knew he was only hanging around to spy on me. Well, Roy took off running, and a big dog from the camp took off after him. That dog did not attack Roy. I saw it with my own two eyes. However, it did scare him, and Roy turned around and cussed that dog for all it was worth. He called that dog cuss words that I didn't even know. The dog was so scared that it ran away, and I knew that I was going to go home and tell on him. That is one thing our parents would not allow us to do, cuss. That was a switching for sure. I could hardly wait to get home. The anticipation of how well I would tell on him was almost more than I could stand. I couldn't decide if I should be sad for the poor dog or mad at Roy. I chose the later.

I walked into the living room, and I said, "Mom, do you know what Roy did?" That was as far as I got. She said, "Yes, Roy told me and your daddy all about it. That dog scared him to death trying to attack and bite him. Roy told us he had said a few words he shouldn't have. He was real sorry. He also said you were going to tell on him. Now, if you have nothing better to do than tattle on your little brother, I will give you something to do. [Oh no; my mind went straight to the kitchen where supper dishes hadn't been done.] No more tattling. I mean it or I will wear you out with a switch."

All of a sudden my head was spinning. How did this get turned around? When did we get that rule? Roy had tattled on me since the day he was born. Now it was outlawed in our house? Well, bully for him. It wasn't fair, but Mom made the rules. Roy sat there looking pathetic and sorry, but I knew down deep inside he was laughing his head off. If I couldn't tell on him, my protection from a snot-nosed little brother was gone. I guess I could write a book on Roy alone. Can't you see how distorted this picture is? Roy did all the sinning, and I got into trouble. I didn't even cuss the dog. I surely would have told on him, though.

I'll never forget the time my cousin Pauline was staying with us while Mom was in the hospital. She was the best babysitter I ever had. Pauline was about sixteen or so. She had the warmest brown eyes you ever looked into. She was very pretty and as spunky as they came. When she dressed up for church, she always looked so nice and ladylike. Pauline quit school to take care of us. She stayed with us for a year and a half until she got married. She knew that she was needed.

Pauline had a big crush on a boy named Clifford Tucker, and he had a big crush on her. One day in the dead of winter, my older brother and a couple of cousins built a big fire out of tires. Clifford came up to hang out with my brother for a while; something he had never done before. Roy went out to stand around the fire with the big boys. I could tell he thought he was pretty special that day. He might have pulled it off, but he had a cold. Pauline looked out the window and said to me, "Go tell Roy to come in the house right now. He has snot clear down on his upper lip. Tell him to come and blow his nose."

I yelled at Roy and told him to come in and blow his nose. I must have burst his bubble because he did what I said, which was pretty good since he had never obeyed me in his life. Pauline found an old rag for him to blow his nose on, and then she threw it into the fireplace. She told him to get a handkerchief out of Daddy's drawer and keep his nose clean. Well the next thing we knew, he had gone back outside. The next time I looked out the window, Roy was wiping his nose for all it was worth. I thought his handkerchief looked a little strange; it didn't look anything like it did when Daddy used one. He had a technique: He would wipe his nose then stuff it back in his pocket. Soon he would pull it out of his pocket again. You could tell he was right proud of himself. He must have felt all grown up.

I kept watching Roy and suddenly it dawned on me that he didn't have a handkerchief at all. He had a sanitary napkin that belonged to Pauline. I said, "Pauline, you had better look here and see what Roy is doing." She took one look out that window and screamed from the top of her lungs. She told Roy to get in the house right now. Poor Roy, he didn't know what she was so mad about, but he come running. Now, Clifford, my brother, and the cousins all knew what Roy had done, and from the sound of Pauline's voice, they knew who it belonged to. They laid down on the ground (not really just a camp kid's expression) and laughed at her. She was ready to murder them all.

I think all the boys secretly had a crush on her. She would go to church with Clifford every Wednesday and Sunday night. My brother Larry and all his friends, like Big Richard and Little Richard, Bill Barnes, and sometimes Clarence Tucker, and others, would climb up in the apple trees [we had four in our front yard] and wait for them to come home. Just about the time Clifford kissed her goodnight, all the boys would make their presence known. They would very loudly pass gas and carry on until Clifford went home and Pauline went into the house. She always got even with them somehow. She told me she could whip the whole bunch at one time. I really believe she could have too.

It was a sad day when Clifford came and got Pauline. He took her away and married her. Just before she left, my mom, dad, and Aunt Thelma decided to have some fun with her. They bought cherries and whipped cream to celebrate her wedding night. Well, bless her heart, she didn't have a clue what they were trying to say. She didn't get the joke until much later when someone explained it to her. She always had a wonderful sense of humor. I never met one person who didn't love her. She was then, and is to this day, the best babysitter that we ever had. I loved her dearly. Not only was she good to me, but if need be, she could also take Larry down a couple of notches. Now Larry was the oldest brother. He didn't mess with us little kids much; he was too old and sophisticated. However, occasionally he would smack me around. That stopped when Pauline came to our house. I walked around like I owned the world. I hoped she would stay forever, and if she should have to leave, I hoped she would take me with her. That wasn't possible, and I missed her a lot.

Pauline once told me that we were too poor to even pay attention. She made me dolls out of clothes pins, and she made me a pretty dress to wear to my grandfather's funeral. She split her own dress down the seams, cut it down to my size, and then sewed it all back together. Now that was sacrifice and love all rolled up together. She will always be my angel. Later in life, Pauline became a registered nurse. She has been taking care of people all her life. I'm sure her experiences at our house taught her a lot.

Larry never seemed to get into any trouble with our parents. The rest of us did, but not Larry. He thought he was in trouble one time though. You see Dad had a few rules that applied to all of us. There was not a deck of cards allowed in our house. Gambling of any form was not allowed: not even penny-ante, as we called it. In addition, we were not allowed to smoke. Cigarettes were off limits and cussing was a huge sin. Now imagine Larry's surprise when he was sitting under the company store porch playing a game of poker with Jody Bartley and smoking a cigarette, and Daddy walked up on him there. Larry wasn't sure how long Daddy had been there before he saw him. He didn't know if he had heard their conversation in which a few cuss words had been passed around. The boys were about thirteen or fourteen years old. Larry said he heard Dad say, "What are you doing, boy?" I think Larry mumbled something like, "Nothing." What a lie. Larry said Dad stayed for a little while, and then he left. I bet Larry died a thousand times while Dad was there.

Larry was afraid to go home, so he stayed out as late as he dared. Imagine how surprised he was when he finally got home, and the only thing Daddy wanted to know was if he was hungry. Dad never mentioned his sins to him again. I know he would have rather had a beating than to see the disappointment in Daddy's eyes. None of us wanted to disappoint our parents. None of the kids in the coal camp wanted to be mean to their parents. We were taught to honor them, and we did. Larry told me that just before Dad died; he asked Dad why he reacted the way he did. Daddy said he thought it was best to just let Larry think about it. It worked, 'cause to this day, Larry can tell you the whole story. It still has the effect Daddy wanted it to have. You can be sure your sins will find you out.

I still remember the evening when Larry came home real early. He hung out with the whole family. He was making sure we all knew he was at home. Every now and again he'd say, "What time is it, Margie?" He acted as though he couldn't tell time. The next day, we all found out why he came home early and made his presence known. Larry had heard some of the older boys planning on breaking into the company store. He wanted to make sure he had an airtight alibi. That's what we were taught to do; if someone was going to do something wrong, we were to come home as fast as we could. It was vital that our parents knew where we were.

My cousin Richard wasn't as smart as Larry. He went along with the guys who broke into the store. He took some cigarettes and candy bars and hid them in Aunt Julia's washing machine. That's where the cops found them the next morning. That was the most excitement we ever had in the Cinco coal camp. Most of us were delighted, me included, until I saw the tears in my uncle Alex's eyes. He didn't go to church for a few weeks. He was too ashamed and hurt to face the people he worshiped with. He felt like a total failure. He couldn't bear the thought that his son would break into the store and steal from it. You see, back in that day, parents took responsibility for their children's actions. Alex felt he had failed to teach Richard right from wrong. As a Christian, that wasn't acceptable to him. Of course, his brothers and sisters in Christ loved him. They prayed for him, and with God's help he would get through it. I believe Richard was sorry. He paid back everything he took. They didn't get any jail time, if they paid their debt to the store, and they did. Some of the older ones did get a little probation.

My uncle Alex was the most humble man I ever knew. He loved God with all his heart. His wife Julia did, too. I'm sure their prayers were answered when Richard didn't go to jail. Richard never got into any more trouble. I'm sure that was an answer to prayer also.

I never will forget the time Mom thought I stole something. You see my cousin Phyllis worked in the company store, and every day or so she would forget and bring her pencil home with her. If she forgot to take it back the next day, she could always get another one. Soon she had a collection of pencils. They were big yellow pencils that had hardly been used. I was at her house one day playing with Linda. We were writing and practicing our spelling. Phyllis had given us both a pencil that was hardly used. When it was time for me to go home, I gave her pencil back, and she said I could have it. That was wonderful, but since it was cold outside, I decided to carry it under my coat to keep my hands warm. When Mom caught me with that big, yellow, hardly used pencil, she thought the worst of me. I tried to tell her I didn't take it and that Phyllis had given it to me. However carrying it under my coat had made me look guilty. Anyhow, Mom made me return it. I cried and my cousin told Mom she had given it to me. Mom told me she was sorry. It all worked out good. That was one nice pencil.

One of my earliest memories about growing up in a coal camp was when we had a little puppy. He had the longest ears I had ever seen on a mutt. We lived in the head of Slate Lick Holler. One morning I went out to play. The puppy kept running and trying to jump up on me. I tried to get away from him, but he was determined to play with me. Finally, I got tired so I started back to the house, and that puppy came after me. I started to run, and he ran with me. He became very excited and bit me on the ankle as I tried to run home. It broke the skin, and that was the end of my patience. I turned and grabbed that puppy and bit down on his long ear as hard as I could. He was yelping in pain, and I wouldn't let go until my dad pulled me off of him. I was about three years old, and Dad said I told the puppy, "If you bite me, I bite back." I don't recall that dog ever bothering me again. I tell you right now, chewing on a dog's ear is not a good thing. I can still taste that ear in my mouth.

Now that puppy wasn't the only one doing any chasing around our yard. I used to love to chase the hens all over the yard. One time I was out in the yard chasing chickens. My dad had just brought home a little red banty rooster. Since I was the boss of that yard, I tried to pick up the new rooster, and to my great surprise, it flogged me. My daddy roared and laughed at that. He said I had finally met my match. To this day, I don't like roosters, especially red ones.

The one incident my mom told me about more often than the

others was when Larry and I went up on the hill to play. As we slid down the hill, I must have slid over a yellow jacket's nest. Larry came down right behind me. I must have moved a rock a little and got them all stirred up, and Larry came behind me and and right into the middle of the swarm. He screamed, and Mom came to our rescue. My clothes were covered with yellow jackets. Larry was getting stung all over. Mom stripped my clothes off me and told me to run, and I did. Mom had dozens of stings up and down her arms. Larry was stung all over. It might be hard to believe, but I didn't get a sting. I believe I had Divine intervention that day.

No matter where we lived, Daddy would find a place to raise chickens, hogs, and a vegetable garden. He really should have been a farmer. One time, Daddy had a hog in a hog pen. I went to visit the stinky thing every day. Imagine my shock when I went down to visit one Saturday, and the hogs head was sitting up on a post. See, Dad was butchering the hog that day. I cried all the way home. I still won't eat pork chops, ham, or sausage. I will occasionally eat bacon, if it's fried real crisp. I guess farm living would not agree with me.

Chapter Five

THE DANGEROUS KID, THE SCARED SISTER, BETSY, AND THE PHOTO

Raymond was the dangerous kid. He was quiet, and he didn't bother anyone. But he had a fiery temper, so you better not bother him. I remember the day he wanted to walk through the kitchen to go out the back door. I had just mopped the floor, and I wouldn't let him walk on it. He got so mad that he threw a mayonnaise jar at me, and it just missed my head and broke all to pieces on the door frame. I went after him, but he could run faster than I could. Raymond was the kind that would knock you in the head and ask questions later.

I remember one time when he chased my cousin around the house with a double-headed ax. I asked him what he thought he was doing, and he told me he would kill our cousin if he laid a hand on him. Seems our cousin had threatened him, and my cousin was a lot bigger than Raymond, but Raymond was a lot meaner. I don't believe that cousin ever laid a hand on Raymond again. I know I wouldn't have.

The only time Raymond would concede that something got the best of him was the day he took on Sally. The story goes something like this. Big-game-hunter Raymond caught himself a flying squirrel. He put it in a cage and hung the cage up on the porch. Judy, our sister, had a cat named Sally. That cat was sitting on the porch banister watching Raymond as he put the squirrel in the cage and hung it up out of harm's way. Sally waited until the time was just right, and she jumped from the banister straight up in the air and knocked the cage to the floor. The door on the cage popped open and the cat got the squirrel. Well, it was on then. Raymond said he screamed and stomped and the cat just ignored him. That is one time he really wanted to kill a cat. Finally, he just had to do something, so he grabbed that cat by the tail and slung it around his head about three times. He was winding up to throw it all the way to Charleston. Something happened about the third trip around his head. Sally got her bearings and went into attack mode. She got her claws into Raymond and scratched up his back, taking skin and shirt with her. Then she took his hat, and a bunch of his hair off his head. She did this all in one swipe. How dare he grab her tail and interrupt her supper? Raymond dropped that cat about six inches away from him and was glad to get rid of her. He got into the house as quick as he could. He had never fought anything as mean as Sally the cat in his life. I think Raymond got a whole new respect for girls that day. Raymond told me that later on someone shot that cat while hunting in the woods. It was an accident. (Sure it was. Shame on you Raymond.)

Raymond might have been dangerous, but he was still the cutest kid ever. He had big brown eyes and dark wavy hair. You couldn't help but adore him. I still do.

Let me tell you about my little sister. Her name was Judy. I named her myself from a *"Jim and Judy"* reader we had in first grade. Judy was little with very straight hair. She was so shy, she would cry if you looked at her the wrong way. She was the love of my life. I was so happy when Mom finally gave me a sister that I went door to door and told all the neighbors.

Since I was big enough to walk my daddy had kept a guitar in my hands. He taught me to play and sing before I started school. I did my first concert when I was in third grade. My teacher was amazed. I thought everyone knew how to do it. Since I was only in third grade, I was still in what we called the little room. It was for first through third grade. My teacher in the little room) had the teacher from the big room (fourth through sixth grade come and hear me play. Since the teacher from the big room had taught my dad in school she wasn't too amazed, because all the Pittman's could do music.

I told you all that so I could tell you about my little sister Judy. She was too shy to sing in front of anyone. Still, she had a booming voice for such a little girl. She could really sing. Being all musical, I devised a plan to get her to open up and sing for everyone; you may recall how Larry got me to learn my lessons when we were playing school. The plan went like this: "Judy, if you don't sing I am going to give you a whipping." We all knew that term in the coal camp. We all got enough whippings. To my joy, it worked. As soon as I threatened her, she would sing. All my friends loved to hear her sing. I was very proud of her, but then I started to feel guilty. I would not have laid a hand on her, but I felt like I had abused her by threatening to. The years went by, and I left the coal camp behind and moved to another state. Judy was in high school, and one day a letter came to me from her. She told me how glad she was that I made her sing. She confessed that she always wanted to sing, but she was so afraid that she couldn't do it. If I hadn't threatened to whip her, she never would have done it. She said, "Today I sing on television, and I am very popular with all the kids in school. Thank you for helping me. I am now the happiest girl in the world." My guilt left, but my pride in her never did.

I need to tell you more about my friend Betsy. She was more fun than a barrel of monkeys. My mother nearly put an end to that friendship. You see, Betsy cussed a little (okay, a lot), and we were never allowed to do that. Most kids in the coal camp did not cuss at our age; besides, I was a churchgoer. One day Betsy's sister asked us to go borrow some salt from my mom. So Betsy and I went after it. We called Mom out to the fence and told her what we wanted. My mom went back in the house and filled up a coffee cup with salt. When she brought it to the fence, she started to hand the cup to Betsy. I don't know to this day what ever possessed me to say this, but I did. I said, "Give me that s*#@'n salt, Jane." Mom didn't say a word; she just handed the salt to me. Boy, did that ever feel good. I knew with a little help, I could be as mean as Betsy. She was fearless. I was beginning to think I was, too. Well, by the time I headed home I thought I might just cuss out the whole family. Before this day, I wasn't allowed to say the "s" word, and you never ever called your parents by their first name. Well, you still didn't if your mother's name was Jane Pittman. I learned a painful lesson when I went home. My sins had found me out. Mom said, You know you are not allowed to use such language as you did, and my name is Mommy to you, not Jane." I still don't like to say either one of those words. When I do, I still feel the sting of Mommy's switch on my legs.

If there was one thing me and Betsy loved, it was bubble gum. (We had quit chewing tobacco.) We would put it in our mouth until there was no more room, and then we let it hang out. We would chew it until all the sweet was gone, and then keep chewing it if we had no more to replace it with. Betsy and I always kept a disgusting mouthful. One night, Betsy went to sleep with her bubble gum still in her mouth. The next morning, her hair was stuck together all over her head. She had lost her bubble gum in the night. Her sister was ready to send her home. I told Betsy not to worry; I had the cure for her. Daddy could cut her hair. My daddy cut all the boys hair that lived in our camp; he might have eight or ten lined up on the front porch the day before school started. The problem was this, he only knew one style, and that was the crew cut. I really think my dad made that style famous. Betsy, her sister, and I told Dad her problem and asked if he could help. He took one look at her and said, "It'll have to be cut short. That's the only way I'll be able to get all the bubble gum out of your hair." Betsy's sister told him to cut it off. She was mad at her for ruining her hair like that. Since Dad didn't cut girls hair, he got out the old clippers, not the scissors, and proceeded to give Betsy a hair cut. Now, mind you, we wore long hair. When Daddy was through, Betsy looked like a boy, and she was ready to kill me. You see, I had kind of promised her that if she had to get her hair all cut off, I would get mine cut the same way; but when I took one look at Betsy's crew cut, I knew my dad was never going to cut my hair. Our friendship kind of grew a little cold after that. What Mommy's switch couldn't do, Daddy's clippers did. They managed to separate me and Betsy. Speaking of bubble gum, well, I still like a piece of that every now and then, and that reminds me of another story.

My brother Raymond had dark curly hair. By the time he was a year old, it had grown down to his shoulders. My mother loved his hair. She liked to say that he took after her. When he got to be one year old, it was time to get a haircut. That was the custom back in the day. His hair was so beautiful that Mom hated to have it cut. It hung in ringlets, she said. She decided to have a photographer come from Charleston and take a picture of him with his curls before she let Daddy cut his hair. It was a big deal to us. Mom was quite proud of the fact that she was having a professional photographer from Charleston take a picture of Raymond. In our coal camp, that was unheard of, and she knew it. So she walked around a little proud for a few days.

Finally the big day arrived and the photographer came out and set up all his equipment. He sat Raymond on a chair. Judy and I were sitting on another chair over in the corner. Raymond, who had no idea what was going to happen to him, got scared and started to cry. I ran over and soothed him and told him it would be fun to have his picture made. I was always trying to mother the younger kids, and most times it worked pretty well. The photographer was very impressed and told me to sit close by in case he needed me to calm Raymond down again. Judy and I moved up a little closer to Raymond and gave him smiles of encouragement. Finally, the picture was taken and Mom must have ordered two hundred wallet-size photos to give to all of our relatives. The day the pictures were due to arrive Mom could hardly wait to see them. She sent me to the post office early that morning. When she opened up the manila envelope, she nearly dropped dead. Raymond was sure enough pretty, but over in the corner the photographer had picked up me and Judy, and we were in the picture. There I sat grinning like a laughing hyena, and the biggest wad of bubble gum you ever saw was hanging out of my mouth. Poor Mommy, she gave every relative we had a copy of that picture, and I have spent years trying to track them all down and get rid of them. Mom sure got revenge on me, and she didn't even use the switch. Judy was smiling too; she had a perm in her hair so it was curly, and she looked real pretty. I'm so glad that Betsy had gone on home because her hair would grow out, but that picture will be around forever. I'm sure she would have tried to put it in the newspaper. Oh, the pain of being a coal camp kid.

Chapter Six

DAVID THE TATTLE TELLER MEETS PEGGY

You have heard about Roy, Raymond, and Judy, and even a little about Larry. But we have another brother named David. David was the cutest little thing you ever laid eyes on. He had blond, curly hair that was thick and long. It was so beautiful that Mommy wouldn't let Dad cut it until he was way past a year old. (Why does God waste that pretty hair on boys? My sister had the straightest hair you ever seen. She could have used Raymond or David's hair.)

Mr. Craigo, who was the company superintendent, came once a month to read our electric meters. David would be out in the yard playing, and Mr. Craigo always patted David on the head and spoke to him. He did that once a month for a long time. Finally, Dad cut David's hair. Mr. Craigo still patted him on the head and spoke to him. One day, Mom just happened to be outside when he came to read the meter, and he asked her where the pretty little blond-headed girl was that used to play out there all the time. Mom laughed and said, "There she is. We just gave him a haircut." Mr. Craigo was a little embarrassed. He shouldn't have been; lots of people made that mistake. That's just how cute David was.

We always called David "the baby" when he was little. That was fine until he got up in the higher grades in school. Then he put a stop to that. We also referred to him as the good brother. He was surely that. David was premature. He only weighed a few pounds at birth, but he had a survivor's spirit. Because of his situation, he had a hearing problem which caused a speech impediment. I loved him more than words could say, and because I took care of him all the time, I got to know his language. Not everyone could understand him when he was little, but I understood every word that came out of his mouth.

As it turned out, David was going to be a tattle teller. Mom broke the rule for him. He was so good all the time that it wasn't bad when he tattled on me. He knew that I was not allowed to smoke. He also knew I sneaked around and made the smoke fly all the time. My cousin Geraldine and I would smoke anything. We started on corn silks and gradually moved up to cigarettes. Every day David assured me he was going to tell Daddy on me when he got home from work that evening. Being that I was a daddy's girl, I couldn't let him do that. Still, he tried and tried with snot and tears, but Dad couldn't understand him. Being his big sister, I laughed at him and teased him until Dad said, "What in the world is he saying?" I sinned again and lied and said, "I don't know." It sounded something like "I dunno." David would cry and repeat over and over, "Daddy, Pocky, mokes." He was saying, "Daddy, Margie smokes."

It wouldn't have been so hilarious if he hadn't been so determined. You would have thought he would give up; not David the survivor. He didn't give up until I stopped smoking in front of him. I told him I quit.

Seems my mouth was always getting me in trouble with David.

One day I told him a dirty joke-not very dirty, just maybe off-color. David never forgot that joke, and every time I got a new boyfriend, David would climb up on his lap and tell him that joke. He would say, "Margie told me a dirty joke; you want to hear it?" He could speak a lot plainer then. They all wanted to hear my joke, and I suffered great humiliation from the baby, the good brother, that I loved so much.

David loved to play the guitar. He spent all the money he had and bought a fancy Fender Telecaster guitar. I think he paid about three hundred and fifty dollars for it. That was a lot of money back then. It had a hard shell case, and it was a beauty. David took good care of his guitar; such good care that later on I'd say a lot later he sold it for four thousand dollars. See, he was not only the baby and the good brother, but he was also smart.

David and his wife Peggy will soon be celebrating forty years of marriage. They are parents and grandparents. When they were five and three, they were best friends. They have a history together. Peggy came to Cinco with her Mother, and they lived just down the road from us. One day as they both were outside, they met and started playing together. They were both little with blond hair. They looked a lot alike at that age. Sometime during their play time, they decided to play on the hill. They were in sight of the house. Peggy's mother eventually came looking for her. Mom went out to help her look. They knew the two were playing together. As the mothers stood in the yard calling for them, David and Peggy hid from them. See they knew that Peggy's mom was going to take her home, and they wanted to keep playing together. They finally came out of the woods where they had been hiding. That's the day that my good brother and his playmate both got a spanking. They got into trouble the first day they met. Now after forty years of marriage, and much more history together, they still want nothing more than to play together. (Go David, Go Peggy). Oh, and by the way, David is still a very good brother.

Chapter Seven

A SHOUTING GRANDMA, SOME GOOD REVIVALS, AND A FUNERAL OR TWO

The only person I ever knew that liked going to church as much as I did was my grandmother. According to her kids, she didn't spare the rod and spoil the child. For years, my mother hated church because of my grandmother. She made them all go to church when they were growing up. They had better not act up in church either; it was God's house, and they were to reverence it. Well I loved her. She taught me more about the bible in a few weeks than I learned in years of being a churchgoer. When she stayed at our house, I shared a bed with her. She would always kneel by that bed and pray before she got into bed. Then she would always tell me bible stories. She made them so real that I could almost see it happening.

When the Baptist church broke out in revival, it was packed every night. Now my grandmother didn't miss no church. She was a shouter and proud of it. She would run the aisles and wave her little handkerchief in the air just like a Pentecostal. She was not ashamed of Jesus. She lived for him every day of her life. He was her life. Church was a big part of all the lives of the coal camp kids. We loved to watch my grandmother carry on, but we would almost bust a gut trying not to laugh at her. Sometimes we just couldn't hold it back. When we did laugh, God must have protected me because the wrath would have fallen on me in a lot of different directions if I'd been caught. My mother would have cut herself a brand new switch to whip me with if she thought I was making a mockery of God. (Some of my grandmother's teaching had rubbed off on her.)

Speaking of that, after we had a good couple of weeks of revival, all of us kids would feel real righteous, and we would hold revival meetings of our own. Now we would sing and shout and testify. We were really into our services. My friend Judy Bartley held them at the schoolhouse sometimes. Her mother was the janitor, and sometimes Judy would go with her to clean. So while she cleaned the little room, we had church in the big room. Since Judy was holding the service, she got to be the preacher. We would have a time praising the Lord just as we saw them do in church. That was the ideal situation, but when that wasn't possible, we would go up on the hill behind my house and have church. I still remember the day my mom caught us. We were letting the hallelujahs fly. I had just proclaimed that "Jesus wept." it was the only bible verse I knew at the time. But I said it with so much feeling that my cousin Linda, who didn't know any bible verses but was in the spirit, shouted, "He sure did." That's about where we were at in the service when Mom appeared. I had sung and shouted until I was hoarse. I could hardly defend myself as Mom accused me of making a mockery of God. I spoke up that day, and I told her no I was not, that I loved God and I really felt everything we were doing. To this day, I believe that was the truth. I believe even if she cut a new switch, I would have still said the same thing. She finally let me off with a stern warning.

After that, when we had church, she didn't stop me. I was just trying to praise God, as I had seen them do in church. She believed I was sincere, even if I was a little dumb. I think God must have told her to leave me be. While we were still in the church mode, if we found a dead bird, we would give it a good Christian funeral. We would sing and cry over that bird just the way we had seen people do over their loved ones. We always made them a casket from a one-pound lard box. Now if it was a long time in between finding dead birds, we would just have to dig one up and give it another good send off. We were coal camp kids, and we created our own fun, and we all liked a good funeral.

Chapter Eight

POINT LICK COAL CAMP KIDS

Growing up was a little hard on coal camp kids, because the kids who didn't live in coal camps tried to look down on us. They might have had more and dressed a lot better, but I promise you they didn't have more fun. When I went to junior high school, things were even better. We met kids from other coal camps then. Some of my favorites were from Point Lick coal camp. They had much better-looking boys than we had. I was starting to notice boys then. I especially noticed Preston Powers. He was the best-looking boy in our class, and he lived up Point Lick. He was a nice boy, too.

My best friend today was from that coal camp. Her name was Bonnie Stone. She was as mean as I was, and she had lots of fun too. Now Bonnie, like me, got along real well with most everybody. There was one exception; Barbara Adkins, a new girl in the camp, who was a lot bigger than Bonnie was the only one she fought with. One day when they were mixing it up, Barbara had Bonnie down on the ground. Bonnie realized she had her good school sweater on;

her mother would be upset with her if she ruined her sweater. She promised Barbara if she would let her go home and take her good sweater off, she would come right back and lay back down and let Barbara be on top again. Barbara fell for it and Bonnie got away. To this day I have to admire the intelligence it took to come up with that. We both regret that we didn't live in the same coal camp, but I believe the good Lord knew a coal camp couldn't take more than one of us, so he split us up.

The Cinco coal camp kids had great church services and revivals and even funerals. Point Lick kids might have done a little better. See Sue Neal (who is now married to Jimmy Stone, Bonnie's brother) had a garage. Not many kids had a garage. She also had a very religious cousin named Patricia. Now five nights a week, they held services in the garage; there was Emma, Mary, and Bonnie (the Stone sisters), Sue Neal, and Cousin Patricia, Merle Horan, and Hazel Powers, Preston's sister. They all attended every night. Patricia was the preacher and the rest of them all got saved every night. They were really big sinners. Now here's where they had it over on us. Patricia would take the whole gang down to the creek and baptize them. Now that was cool. No two ways about it, they had us beat when it came to having church. You see none of us were ever baptized. I don't know why exactly, but I'm guessing we couldn't find enough water in the little creek that ran by our house.

When it came to funerals, I really believe we loved our birds more, because Bonnie and her gang would have funerals for anything that died. They buried turtles, frogs, fish, and other things. Then, after a few days, they would dig them up and throw them at each other. They desecrated the graves of their critters; we only dug up a bird if we were desperate for another funeral. We always reburied them with all due respect. I believe we were more respectful of our dead.

They probably had more fun, though. Bonnie's brother Steve once threw a dead turtle and hit Linda Adkins in the head. When it hit her, it busted all to pieces. Bonnie said it was so rotten it should have stayed in the ground. Bonnie got a little bit of rotten turtle on her dress, which stunk really bad, but even after they washed Linda's hair every day and sometimes more than once a day, she still carried that stink around with her for a month. (Poor Linda; shame on you, Steve.)

I don't know if you have realized it or not but it seemed if there was meanness going on Steve would be in the middle of it. In Point Lick, all the trouble seemed to follow Steve.

Bonnie's Aunt Mary came to visit for Christmas one year. You see Aunt Mary liked a little drink once in awhile. She had left her whiskey in the car because Bonnie's dad didn't allow it in the house. Steve (Bonnie's brother who was about nine years old at the time) knew Aunt Mary had a fifth of whiskey in the car. On the pretense of going after buckets of coal, Steve would go get him a big drink of whiskey. After a few times of doing this, he had drunk all he could hold. Well, guess what? Steve got drunk and went into the house. He laid down under their Christmas tree and fell asleep. Soon there was a little trickle of water coming out from under the tree. You see, Steve was peeing on the presents. (Merry-hiccup-Christmas, everyone.)

Lenny Ulbrich was in all of our classes at school. Lenny, Judy Bartley, and I grew up together. He was the only decent-looking boy in Cinco except our brothers. I loved Lenny like a brother. We grew up together; we knew each other. No courting would ever happen between us. Well, I found out later that Judy Bartley had played post office with him and they had done some kissing. Imagine that.

Lenny had a crush on my cousin Norma. When he got a job in the company store, we would drop in every afternoon and get an ice-cold Pepsi-Cola. I can still taste that drink; it was so good. Now the best part was that Lenny never took our money. He treated us every day. Norma wouldn't go to the store alone, so I always went with her. Free Pepsi-Cola, that was worth going for. When Norma moved to Michigan, I never saw her again.

When I go to the cemetery to decorate Mom and Dad's graves,

there are two little graves that I cry over every time. You see Mom gave birth to eight children, and two of them died as infants. I was in between the two brothers that died. I still cry for the life they might have had. I have had survivor's guilt most of my life. My friend Bonnie says that God had a work for me to do, that's why I was spared. I sure do thank Him for heaven. One day I will meet my little brothers there.

Lenny's mom and dad had a houseful of kids, too. He had one sister for us to play with. Her name was Judy, also. When Lenny's cousins lost their mom, they had to move from Point Lick to Cinco. They moved in with Lenny's family. His mother took good care of them. That's the way people were in the coal camp. No kids were thrown away. Ida Ulbrich raised those three children as her own. In an already crowded household, there was always room for three more. There was Mary Lou, Barbara, and Billy. Mary Lou was beautiful and all the boys had a crush on her. She also played my maid in the Christmas play. When she got to junior high school, she was a majorette. We were proud of her. At least one girl from Cinco had made it big. (Go Mary) Later on, Judy Ulbrich became a majorette also.

Larry and I, because of our age difference, didn't do too many things together. We did, however, have a fishing experience. When the creek got low, the little fishes in the creek were easy to catch. One day we got a big bunch of them. I don't know whose bright idea it was to have a fish fry, but we did. We had both seen Mom cook fish that Dad had caught, but I don't think we ever seen them clean the fish. So I rolled them in corn meal and used a cast-iron skillet and had the grease so hot it was popping. It's a thousand wonders I didn't catch myself on fire. I was cooking on a coal stove. It was hot, and I wasn't very big. We cooked up the biggest mess of fish that anyone had ever seen, guts and all. I don't remember us eating them, but the Lord knows Raymond or Roy would have eaten them in a heartbeat. We weren't trying to poison anyone, we just decided to have a fish fry. Kids in coal camps come up with these great ideas sometimes.

Larry and I were also somewhat enemies. He was bigger and stronger than me. I couldn't fight him; he was too big. One day a girl came to our coal camp for a visit. Her name was Ellen Mullins. She had a king-size crush on Larry. Well Ellen and I got to be friends, and she told me some really good stuff on my brother. I never did know for sure if it was true, but at last I had an equalizer. He knew I'd tell on him and Ellen Mullins. Ducky was her nickname; I never knew why. As she got older, we called her Ellen. That girl could give you some good information. I'm still not sure if Larry had a crush on her or not.

Chapter Nine

DEATH IN A COAL CAMP; I STILL MISS EFFIE

The saddest day of my life was when death came to Cinco. My cousin Effie drowned in Coal River. She was only thirteen at the time. I was totally devastated. My aunt Thelma and uncle Sidney were never the same after Effie drowned. It seems my uncle Sidney told Effie she couldn't go swimming in that river. Since he and Dad fished there quite often, he was very familiar with the dangers of the river. Although she would be with her two older sisters and their boyfriends, Sidney still said it was too dangerous for Effie.

Soon after their conversation, Sidney laid down and fell asleep on the couch. When Effie asked Thelma if she could go swimming, not realizing the danger, Thelma told her to go on. It seemed that Sidney kind of blamed Thelma for her death. It wasn't her fault, but it really hurt to see the pain in our family. During the time of the wake, Thelma kept passing out. They had to call the doctor. She went into epileptic seizures. It was very sad.

My aunt and uncle had Effie's wake in their living room. I went to see her. I sat right near Effie's coffin until Mom made me go home. I know now that I was traumatized. It was the first time I had seen death face to face. It is ironic that I phrased it like that, because a song called "Face to Face" was Effie's favorite song. They sang it at her funeral. Poor Thelma had to be carried from the church. It was the saddest day I can recall in Cinco.

Effie played with us all the time. She was older, but she would still take time to help us build a playhouse out of rocks, bricks, and tin cans. Effie had beautiful long wavy hair. She was so pretty. For years after she died, I would have nightmares about her. I would dream she was calling me to come and play. She would always have her back turned to me, and I could see her long, beautiful hair. When she turned around, her face was that of a skeleton. It almost drove me crazy. I woke up my mom more than once crying for Effie. I think it was about that time that I stopped having funerals for the birds. It was too painful. I will always miss her. Years later, Sidney and Thelma divorced.

All of us kids loved swimming in the big creek. When it came a good hard rain, it was perfect for a dip. Mom had forbidden me to go in the big creek unless my older brother was there also. Well, one hot summer day I couldn't resist the temptation. All my little friends were in the creek, and soon I was too. I had on shorts and a T-shirt. After a wonderful day of frolicking in the creek, I sat in the sun and let my hair and clothes dry. I decided that Mom would never know I had been in the creek. There was no need to tell on myself. When I got home Mom said, "I told you not to get in the big creek without your brother with you. Since he has been home all day, I know he wasn't with you. Young lady, you are in trouble." I tried to lie my way out of it, but I had long blond hair; it was real wavy, and when it dried without brushing, it had a way of tangling up. My pretty hair was a dead giveaway. My mother could look at you and know when you were lying. Needless to say, she sent me after a switch that day for sure.

Coal Miner Jesse Pittman My dad

My Mom Jane Pittman

The Sophisticated Older
Brother Larry Pittman

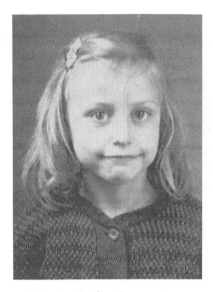

Future Author Songwriter
Margie Pittman

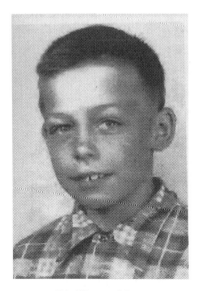

Big Hearted Roy

Big Game Hunter
Raymond Pittman

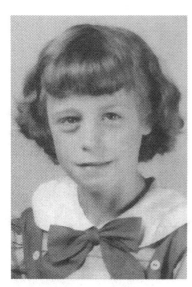

Sweet Little Sister
Judy Pittman Quentrill

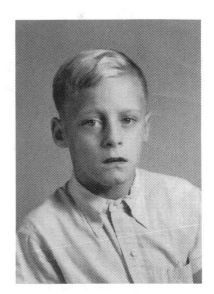

The Baby David Pittman

Dad's worst nightmare
Emma Stone Johnson

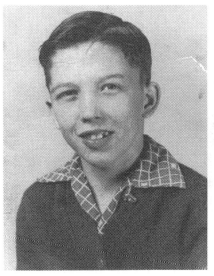

Always in the center of
trouble Steve Stone

My Best Friend Forever
Bonnie Stone Jarrett

Steven Stone, Marvin Horan, Carlie Horan

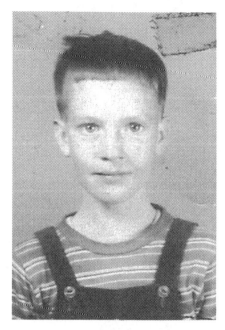

Future Reverend Edward (Red) Jarrett

Be careful what you pray for
Bonnie Stone Jarrett

David Pittman and Peggy Elswick Pittman
at about the age they first met,
now married 40 years

Cinco Company store

Point Lick Four Room Schoolhouse

The Cinco coal camp as seen from the mouth of Slate Lick Hollow in 1919. COURTESY HAROLD FIELD

Cinco Coal Camp @1919

Campbells Creek Mine No. 4 At Rensford, West Virginia

Campbells Creek Locomotive

Coal Cars Being Loaded at a Tipple

Chapter Ten

GOING TO THE DOCTOR AND OTHER TALENTS

If there was one thing us coal camp kids had, it was a good company doctor. Ours was Doctor Crawford. He was the best. I used to go see him at least once a week. I always told him I had a cold and needed some cherry cough syrup. Doctor Crawford gave me a bottle that he would refill with cherry syrup. He would get a big kick out of me forcing a good cough so I could get a refill.

But that was not the only reason I went to the doctor. One time I was convinced I had the "yellow jaundice." I told Doctor Crawford all about my symptoms. I said, "Look in my eyes; the whites are yellow. My skin is turning yellow, and Doctor Crawford, [I whispered this part] I even pee yellow." He thought that was the funniest thing he had ever heard. Still, he gave me a bottle of pills [vitamins, I think]. He said to tell my daddy I should have some candy and all the fruit juice I could drink until it cleared up. Mom was in the hospital and

Doctor Crawford made a special trip to tell her of my latest illness. That doctor was sometimes amazed at my diagnoses, like the time I took my cousin in and informed the doctor she had the seven-year itch, and she did. I further advised him that I didn't want to get it. I must have heard my mother say that. Well, the good doctor took care of our dilemma. She smelled like sulfur for a while, and then she was okay.

I could look at a poison ivy plant and break out all over. When that happened, the doctor would come to the house and give me a shot to clear it up. Sometimes I would invent a little disease just so I could go and talk to the doctor. I took all my brothers and my sister for their immunization shots for school. They wouldn't cry if I promised them a sucker. The doctor always kept a drawer of them somewhere in that office. Judy Bartley took her little brothers too. I don't know if she got a sucker or not. In the coal camp, the older sister did a lot of things that their mothers should have done. It was a way of life for us.

Doctor Crawford was a good man and an excellent doctor. He brought a lot of joy to the coal camp kids. Sometimes a trip to the doctor's office was the highlight of my day. If I got my bottle of cough syrup, the good feeling could last a couple of days, if I sipped it slowly.

I remember when we were in the seventh grade, the music teacher, who was also my homeroom teacher, announced she was having a talent show. My dear friend Judy Bartley informed the teacher that I could sing and play the guitar. Well, of course the good teacher wanted me to sing in the talent show. I really didn't want to, but I finally agreed if Judy would sing with me. We practiced that song until it was perfect. The teacher decided to have a little boy in our classroom do the sound effects. It went like this: Judy and I would sing, "How much is that doggie in the window?" and the sound effect was a "woof woof." now, wasn't that nice.

When the big night arrived, Judy was a no-show, and I had to sing alone. At first, I knew I would be mad at her for life. I was so embarrassed. But being a true musician, I knew the show must go on. Well I won't call any names, but there was a boy in the audience that I had a crush on forever, and he was looking at me like he admired what I was doing. That took the sting of embarrassment right away. He even spoke to me after that. Of course, after the music teacher found out I had a little talent, I had to sing in the glee club. I wasn't too happy about that. I still wish Judy had sung with me. "How much is that doggie in the window?" never sounded prettier.

I had an admirer now, though, and I wasn't mad at Judy anymore. I reasoned it out like this: if Judy had been there, he might have admired her instead of me. I decided it was fate which kept her home, not fear. It was not until I started writing this book that I discovered that we had a crush on the same boy. Judy asked me if we ever fought over him. I said no. I didn't know she liked him, and she didn't know I liked him. You learn something new every day. Now wasn't that a coincidence? Everyone will want to know his name. Well, his first name was Ralph, and that's all I'm saying.

Judy Bartley was a beautiful girl. She always wore her hair long. It was wavy like mine, except maybe a little more manageable. She had dark hair and eyes. She could get any boy she wanted. When the one she wanted came along, she married him, and they were married forty-nine years. That must have been love. Carl was his name, and he is in heaven now.

Chapter Eleven

HOLIDAYS, TV, HOUSEWORK, AND SUPERSTITIONS

All of the holidays were fun in that two-room schoolhouse. We made hearts for Valentine's Day. We also gave each other valentines. We got them at the company store so they were all alike. Christmas was, of course, our favorite holiday. We didn't get a lot of toys by today's standards, but we were happy to get anything. My dad was always the church Santa Claus. We always got a fruitcake from the church to show their appreciation. My daddy had a really good "Ho, Ho, Ho," and all my friends were a little envious of me having Santa for my daddy. After a while, they knew better. My glory days were over by the time I was seven.

The holiday that stands out in my mind the most in the coal camp was Halloween. We always had a bar of soap just in case somebody got stingy with us and wouldn't treat us. Some people said to go ahead and soap their windows, they needed cleaning anyway. We were happy to oblige them. It was more fun to do bad things without permission, but when we got permission, we would still milk it for all it was worth.

In West Virginia, the fall weather can be a little unpredictable. One year I remember putting on my costume to go trick-or-treating. It was not heavy or bulky. We mostly wore masks, and they were all alike since they were purchased at the company store. This particular night stands out in my mind because I didn't have enough clothes on to keep me warm. I nearly froze to death. "Do you think I went home to get a sweater or a coat? Not on your life." That was the one night of the year you could get free candy. I would have stayed and collected candy until I froze into an icicle. As a result of that, the next year I bundled up, and it was a warm fall evening and I almost burned up. Oh well, it was still a productive night.

We measured success by how much candy we got. The best Halloween I remember was the year I soaped Mommy's windows and she had a fit. While she was handing out treats, I sneaked around to the back of the house and I was tricking her. She said she had just cleaned her windows; they didn't need cleaning. When I was through, there were a couple that did need cleaning. I never confessed that to my mother. She would not have seen the humor in it at all. As mad as she was at "The little devil" that did it. I thought: I'll have to carry this secret to my grave. I never did it again, but I'll have that memory for years to come.

We didn't do much harm; maybe a tree across the road and that was mostly done by the older boys. I remember when a group of boys got together and shoved over Ruby Bartley's outhouse. I was going to be upset with them; we all loved Ruby. She was very good to us kids. Then she told us she had put the boys up to it. Seems she needed a new outhouse, and the only way she could get the company to build her a new one was to get rid of the old one. Ruby thought it was funny. I did too. What if someone had been using it and the boys pushed it over with them in it? That would have been even funnier. Later on, when

I thought about it, I realized that Ruby was one smart lady. She was the only one I ever knew that outsmarted the coal company. Nobody ever told on the boys, and Ruby was pearly white. Her name was never mentioned. She got a nice, new toilet out of the deal, and the boys had a ball doing something mean with permission. I'm almost sure Larry played a role in that mischief.

One time Judy and Louise Pennington went walking up the road looking for boys. They stopped long enough to block the road because some of the older boys had cut down the trees. Judy and Louise were teenagers then and thought they were all grown up. After they blocked the road, they walked on up the road as though they were innocent. A couple of boys walking up the road behind them went on by the road block. Just about that time, a deputy sheriff pulled up and the boys got into trouble and had to move the road block. The girls never looked back. They just looked like two cool chicks. Now wasn't that cold? Oh well, in the coal camp girls had to be tough, and they were. We went from mean little kids to tough teens, but we never did anyone any harm. However, if we had the opportunity to be a little mean to the boys, we couldn't always resist.

The day after Halloween, Judy and I climbed on the school bus to go to school. Two boys from up at Ten Mile trying to look down on us, said, "Halloween is over; you can take off your false face now." They were not our friends, not then, not ever. The way we looked at it, they had no more than we did, and they weren't nearly as pretty. Everyone knows that pretty may be only skin deep, but ugly goes all the way to the bone, and they were ugly.

Sometimes our bus was so crowded that we couldn't all find a seat. In times like this, we had to sit on each others' laps. Judy informed me that I sat on her lap. I said, "Well, I didn't weigh nothing, so I guessed I didn't do you any harm." I had to sit somewhere and that was as good a place as any. Judy was a good friend to me.

Ruby was Judy's mother. Judy had two sisters; Emogene was the oldest. Just like Judy, she was as pretty as any movie star I had ever seen. She had a beautiful smile. She was real nice. The baby sister, called Cookie, was so young that we didn't play with her. Now Emogene would serve as a flower girl when there was a funeral. She collected ribbons from the flowers she carried to the cemetery. She had a drawer stuffed full of them. She didn't have to worry about Judy stealing any of them. When she found them, it gave her the creeps and scared her.

Judy, like me, had a bunch of brothers. The oldest one was named Claude. I had a mean crush on him, but I never told anyone then. Now I'm telling everyone. Jody was her brother, and he was famous for breaking bones. Every time you saw Jody, he had a new cast. We did appreciate his breaks. See if he broke his right arm, he didn't have to write until the cast came off. How lucky was that/ Just think how cool he would have looked if he came to school on crutches with a broken leg and a cast on his right arm; we would have really respected that. Then there was Jerry, and Roy, and they played with my brothers all the time. They were good kids.

We were among the first in our coal camp to get a television. It was a twenty-one-inch black-and-white. It got three channels if Daddy had the antenna right. He had put it on the top of the mountain so we could get reception. Every time it rained, the TV would get all snowy. Dad would go back to the top of the mountain. One of the brothers, usually Larry, would go halfway up the hill, and we at the house would yell to them what the TV was doing. Dad didn't mind going on Friday or Monday; those were the two nights that me and Daddy watched the fights. Gillette razor blades sponsored them. The Monday and the Friday night fights came on at nine o'clock, and me and Daddy always rooted for the underdog. I don't know if I really liked the fights, or if I just liked spending time with Daddy. However, I learned enough to do a little boxing in our back yard with my brothers and cousins. I was real good for a girl, Daddy said.

Every Saturday morning, the little boys from the camp all came to our house to watch cartoons on our television. Well I was at the age where I tried to keep the living room clean just in case a boyfriend dropped by. Every Saturday, Mom would make me wait until the cartoons went off before I could clean the living room. She'd say, "Now, Margie, you leave them little boys alone. They are not bothering anything." Of course, she was right, and I was wrong. Today I laugh about it, but back then it wasn't very funny. Everywhere a little boy sat there was chunks of mud. You see the camp stayed muddy, and when the boys walked to our house, they couldn't stay out of it. They would all politely leave when the cartoons were over. I would clean up their mud and soon the living room would be presentable.

If there was one thing I hated about housework, it was doing the dishes. We had a big dishpan that we filled with water, and one person washed and the other dried if there were two working together. Judy and I were supposed to do the supper dishes. It was our job. Well, I had a Kodak camera that Judy really wanted. I would tell her that if she would wash the dishes, I would give it to her. I did give it to her, but then I'd take it back. This went on for some time. One day I guess my guilt caught up with me, and I gave it to her for good. She told everyone how mean I was to her over that camera. Finally, she even said she really didn't want it anyhow. Well, I wouldn't have washed all those dishes for ten cameras.

The hardest part about the dishes was having to wash Daddy's dinner bucket. In the mines, it was easy to dent their buckets. In every dent, the coal dirt would accumulate. It was oily and it stuck like glue. That made it really hard to clean. I hated that job so much that I would beg mom to wash it for me. She said no, that it was my job. A few times I hid it in the bottom of the cabinet. When Mommy found it the next morning, she had to wash it before she could pack Daddy's lunch. I think she must have given me the benefit of the doubt by thinking I had just overlooked it. By the third time I tried that little trick, she got as mad as a hornet and let me know that it had better not ever happen again. That was when I had to start bribing Judy into washing the dishes. I had a beautiful doll that I had won by taking the most people to church. Judy did a lot of dishes for that as well. I didn't even want the doll, but it sure came in handy. Judy was happy with the doll and the camera, and I was glad I didn't have to do dishes for a long time.

Bonnie had a different technique for getting out of doing dishes. See being the baby of her family, she had two older sisters. All she had to do was pick a fight, and they would run her out of the kitchen. It was easier to do them without her help than to fight with her. Now that was smart except for the day her daddy caught her. That time, when Mary told her to go on out and play and she would do the dishes, her daddy said no. He told Mary to go out and play, and Bonnie had to do the dishes all by herself. She really suffered that day. I guarantee she had dishpan hands. I don't know if she did it again or not, but if she did, I believe she would have been too smart to let her daddy catch her.

I finally asked Judy Bartley how she got out of washing dishes. She said she cleaned all the rest of the house, and her mother washed the dishes. I would have gladly done that, but Mom put them dishes on me and Judy. I don't mean to criticize my mom. She worked harder than anyone I ever knew. Raising six kids in a coal camp was not easy for anyone. She cooked and washed our clothes and did all the rest. It shouldn't have hurt me and Judy to wash supper dishes. I would still hate to wash that old dinner bucket.

Beverly Marshall actually said she didn't mind doing dishes. Can you believe that? As a matter of fact, she still likes to wash dishes. What's wrong with that girl?

I remember a few times when we had to eat out of pie and cake pans. You see Roy liked to climb up in Mommy's dish cabinet. A few times he turned it over and broke every dish we had. He was mean that way. The one thing that would stop him dead in his tracks was an onion. He hated the feel of onions. If there happened to be one in the cabinet anywhere, Roy would move on to something else. He wouldn't chance touching that onion. I think Mom finally resorted to keeping her onions in the bottom of her dish cabinet. Nothing was safe from Roy except the onions.

One night as a group of us kids were playing, we came up with a new game. We would take two tin cans and stomp our feet into them so we could walk on the cans. A boy named Harry Jackson was playing with us. He was one of Larry's best friends. He was a very nice boy. He went to stomp a can, and it flipped up in the air and hit Roy in the head. Now Roy could be the drama king at times; he went squalling to Mom and Dad. He told them that he was just standing out there looking up at the buttermilk sky, minding his own business (as though Roy ever minded his own business; he was too busy minding mine), and Harry Jackson hit him in the head with a tin can. At the time there was a song out called, "Oh, Buttermilk Sky." Roy borrowed the name to dramatize his story. Of course, Mom and Dad knew what we were doing, and they knew it was an accident. Still, they had to laugh at Roy's wonderful explanation of the event. They thought he was cute. I personally thought he needed a switching for lying about Harry. I had a childhood crush on him. He died shortly thereafter. I missed him for a long time. He called me margarine butter, so I would chase him.

We did have a few superstitions in the coal camp. Boyce Winfree told Roy Bartley how to get rid of a wart. See you had to steal the oldest dish rag your mother had and wrap it around a sand rock and rub it on the wart. Next, you buried it in the ground, and you never told anyone where it was buried. The wart would leave in a few days, but if you told where the dish rag was buried, it would come back.

Boyce gave Roy a duck egg, and he took it and put it in Pa-Pa Landers' chicken's nest so he would think his chickens laid that big egg. It was at least twice as big as a hen egg. I'm sure Pa-pa knew better, but it was one more good joke as far as the boys were concerned. They knew Pa-Pa Landers would just enjoy their joke. He was a good person. You see coal camp kids took their fun wherever they could find it.

Bonnie told me some good superstitions from their coal camp. I remember a few of them: if you break a mirror you get seven years of bad luck; if you step on a crack, you'll break your mother's back: walking under a ladder was real bad; if you spilled salt, you had better throw some over your left shoulder to ward off bad luck. No wonder Bonnie wanted to marry a preacher. She did need someone to keep her in line. This was a favorite: don't ever let a black cat run out in front of you. That would be instant bad luck unless you turned around and went back to the next curve. Then turn back and go the way you started. There were many more, but I don't have the room to print them all. We grew up on superstition and fortune-telling. But the most important thing in our lives was God, and He protected us from our silliness. We believed Him above everything else, and we still do.

Judy said Roy was the good kid in her family, like David was in ours. It's my opinion they all have a few cracks in their armor. I found David's when he tried to tell on me for smoking. That wasn't a nice thing for a good kid to do. I could have gotten into serious trouble with my dad. I also had to add a few more sins. I lied to my dad when I said that I didn't know what David was saying. I'll tell you the truth; if Jesus hadn't loved me enough to die for those sins, I would bust hell wide open. I'm so thankful for my Savior.

When I told this to Judy, she agreed that Roy was a tattle teller too. That's the problem with good kids; they tell on you, and you can't get even with them. They are just too stinking good.

Judy also reminded me of how we used to fuss and fight one minute and play together the next. She said she thought she had been a hateful kid. I don't remember her that way at all. She just had a mind of her own, and she knew how to use it. I still can't believe she used to play post office with Lenny Ulbrich. He was as cute as they come, but so was Judy. (You go, girl!)

Chapter Twelve

COUSIN NORMA, BROTHER LARRY, AND ROY GOES FISHING

My cousin Norma Jean and I went up on the hill and found us a grapevine. It was long enough to swing on, and we did. We had so much fun swinging out over the hill. Norma caught her pants pocket in a tree once and like to never got it loose. She was dangling in midair. She looked so funny, I had to laugh. She was screaming at me to help her, and there was no way I could reach her. Finally, her pocket came loose, and she swung all afternoon after that. We were a fearless bunch.

One day my big brother Larry came up on the hill to see what we were doing. When he caught us on that swing, he swore it would break with us on it and we could break our neck. What he did then was nothing short of a tragedy. He took out his pocket knife and cut our grapevine so short that none of us could reach it anymore. What can I say? That was a brotherly act of some kind; I'm not sure if it was kindness or revenge. Who knows? The woods were always a favorite place for us to play.

Just think how this next episode must have pleased me. See Larry had to use the bathroom while in the woods one day. He couldn't wait until he got home. That happens sometimes when you're in the woods. So, what do you do? You use the bathroom in the woods. So he did, but he didn't have any paper with him, so he used leaves instead. Well, Larry got a hold of the wrong kind of leaves. After a little while, he started itching where it is hard to scratch. Soon he was in misery. He was itching to death. It seems Larry had used poison ivy instead of paper. He was highly allergic. Larry was a mess. He was broken out all over. He missed about a week of school. Now the doctor needed to visit him. I wasn't the only one who needed Doctor Crawford to come to my rescue. He gave Larry a shot, and he finally started getting better. Larry never made that mistake again. Even coal camp kids can learn a lesson if they have to. I feel sure he knew he had to. (Way to go Larry)

Speaking of brothers, how many women remember when bicycles were only bought for the boys. Girls didn't get bicycles; we got dolls. See it was a known fact that girls would marry, have children, and be homemakers. (Not!) It wasn't ladylike to ride a bicycle in a dress. (We all wore dresses at that time.) My brother Roy had a dandy bike; red and shinny and every time I tried to ride it Roy would throw rocks at me. Sometimes he even hit me. One time when he cracked me on the ankle, I cried and told Daddy. He was not too sympathetic to me since I was trying to ride off on Roy's bike. That was stealing, and Roy was just defending his property against a thief. I remember him always getting onto Roy about throwing rocks at the little birds. I guess sisters didn't count. Now Roy could really throw a rock. He was very accurate. One day he threw a rock at a bird and knocked it right out of the air. I don't remember for sure, but we probably gave it a good funeral.

There was one boy in our camp that was too sweet for words. Like

I said, girls were never given bicycles. However, this nice kid named Curtis Mack would let me ride his bicycle as much as I wanted to. He trusted me to take care of it, and I did. Curtis is a minister now. That doesn't surprise me. He was born with a Christian heart. He suffered a great tragedy when we were growing up. His mother Irene died while having surgery, and we were all devastated. I remember going door to door and collecting money to buy flowers from our camp. Everyone gave to that fund. We always did that when there was a death. I usually helped collect for it. We would take the money to Ida Ulbrich, and she and her daughter Norma would see to it that flowers were sent to the funeral. The Macks were real good people, and we wanted to show them our love. Soon after his mother's death, Curtis moved away. I really missed him. He was a true friend.

If I held the title of being Daddy's girl, well, Roy could certainly qualify as Daddy's boy. I remember one day when I went back to school after my lunch break without Roy. I told the teacher that Roy was sick that afternoon and couldn't come to school. She said, "Are you sure he is sick?" I said, "Yes." Well, she said, "I just saw your dad headed for the creek with his fishing pole and Roy was sneaking right behind him." This is how Roy followed Dad. He would give Dad a head start, and then he would follow far enough behind so Daddy wouldn't see him and run him back to the house. By the time Dad got to the fishing hole, Roy was right behind him, so he would go ahead and let him stay and fish with him. Like I said, he could always get me in more trouble than I could ever get out of. Mrs. Palmer surely thought I was lying. Mommy told me that Roy was sick and wouldn't be going to school in the afternoon. I guess he was faking an illness because Dad was home that day. The truth is, Roy loved to hang around Dad. I guess we all did. I couldn't even fault him for that. After all, he was a practicing coal camp kid. A day with Dad was far better than a day with the teacher. Grades were never that important to Roy anyway.

Chapter Thirteen

CINCO WAS LIVING UP TO IT'S NAME AND MY FAVORITE AUNT THELMA STORIES

I believe that I told you our coal camp was called Cinco and we pronounced it sinco. My mother always said it sure lived up to its name. It was the most sinful place she had ever seen. She often said she wished the old beer joint would burn to the ground. I'm glad she never told that to Raymond, or he, might have carried out her wishes. He was a good kid that way. According to Mom all the bad people hung out at the beer joint. I don't really know what category Mom was in. She didn't go to the beer joint, so I'm not sure she was a sinner. She didn't go to church either. I think she was what is known as a rebellious child. I guess she thought it was spiteful to my grandmother if she refused to go to church. I think she had some misplaced anger. However, she finally gave her heart to Jesus and she was the best Christian I ever knew. I never heard her cuss again.

Let me tell you about my aunt Thelma. Everybody loved Thelma. She was as round as she was tall. She had a special gift; she could tell your fortune and sometimes get it right. That took some kind of gift. I do not think the gift was of God, because when she was saved she could not do it anymore. However, many nights all her women friends and relatives would go to Aunt Thelma's house and wait in line for her to tell their fortunes. This is how it went. Aunt Thelma would brew up a big pot of coffee. She would put the grounds right in the water, and when she poured them a cup it always had some grounds in the cup. They would drink their coffee and turn their cup upside down in the saucer and then turn it three times. Aunt Thelma would read the grounds left in the cup. She read mine a few times, and some of it did come true. At least, I thought it did. Judy Bartley told me that Thelma had read her fortune also. I don't know if hers came true or not.

Fortune teller or not, my aunt Thelma was the best cook around. She made the best squirrel gravy in the camp. She could make a hot dog that would melt in your mouth. We always picked blackberries together. I would get a good dose of poison ivy every time we did it, but I would do it anyway. She would can the blackberries and make cobbler with them in the winter. She always gave me some. One time they caught a turtle, and she made turtle soup. She offered me some of that, but I declined. She also made oyster stew, and I turned that down too. Like I said, she could cook.

The only time I ever got upset with my aunt Thelma was when Daddy killed my chicken. See it was like this, we had a chicken that was crippled. I named her Gladys and claimed her for my own. I really liked that chicken; I guess because I saw her as the underdog and I always went for the underdog. Well, Gladys grew up quite happy. I saw to it that she was well fed. (What a mistake) One Sunday morning when Daddy went out to kill a couple of chickens for Mom to fry up for dinner, he got Gladys. He didn't know that Gladys had become my pet chicken until he told Mom he had killed the one with the crippled foot, and I heard him. I cried and went straight to my aunt Thelma to tell her the awful news about Gladys. Something must have struck her funny, because as hard as she tried, she could not help but laugh at my dilemma. She finally got control of herself when she saw how upset I was. She tried to comfort me by telling me that Gladys was in chicken heaven; she wouldn't be crippled anymore. I told her that wasn't true; in a few minutes, she was going to be in the belly of my aunt and uncle who came for dinner. Thelma sympathized with me then. I guess I wasn't upset with her anymore.

My aunt Thelma was one of a kind. She kept the company store in business. Uncle Sidney had a bill at the company store. You know credit. Thelma run it up so high that he would never get it paid off. A young girl name Janice worked in the store at the time I am going to tell you about. She worked days, so Aunt Thelma sent me to get her some panties. Well, I wasn't very old so it went like this: "Hey, Janice, Thelma told me to come down here and get her some bloomers. She said to tell you to send her the biggest pair in the store. They ought to fit." Everybody started laughing because the store was full of coal miners: dirty old men. Janice was embarrassed to death. See I was yelling it at the top of my lungs because I didn't want to forget what she had told me to get. I was responsible that way. Since they were good friends, Janice went and had a little talk with my aunt Thelma about my language. My aunt Thelma just laughed and told Janice I had done exactly what she told me to do. Janice said to write a note the next time and don't tell her what is in it. (Well bully for you girl, I could read really good. And besides aunt Thelma couldn't read or write. I did all her writing for her.)

When Thelma's daughter moved to Michigan with her husband, I had to write letters to her from Thelma. It seems like yesterday when I would hear her calling me, and she would say, "Hey, Margie Doodle, come down and write me some letters. I made you some hot dogs." That's all it took, I would have written letters all day for just one of those. Aunt Thelma is gone now, but some of my best memories growing up in the coal camp were about her. I will always miss her.

Chapter Fourteen

ROCK-AND-ROLL CAME TO CINCO

The company store was the focal point of the community. You could get your candy, bubble gum, Pepsi, and some scrip if you needed money. Two nights a week, you could go to a movie in the basement. It didn't get much better than that, we thought.

Then one day the word came to us that someone had taken over the little store down the road and turned it into a place for teenagers to hang out. It would be open Friday and Saturday nights. We knew it couldn't get better than that. There was a juke box with all the latest songs on it: Elvis, Marty Robbins, Patsy Cline, and every body else you could think of. Dick Clark had *American Bandstand* on TV, and we watched it every afternoon. We learned to dance. We did the jitterbug and waltzed all night long; well, until around ten, when we had to go home. Judy Bartley and I made the rounds. We could dance and that was all we went for, that and the cute boys that would come up from one of the other coal camps. We called the store the "Green Lizard" 'cause the building was painted green. I think my cousin

Richard came up with that name and it stuck. We had a lot of fun there. We probably got our hearts broken too at times, but it all went with growing up.

Remember when Elvis first came on the scene, shaking his hips and singing that sinful music our parents didn't like. We loved him, swinging hips and all. I spent all my babysitting money on Elvis records, Elvis movies, and the juke box. The fifties were great. Now my dad was a good musician, so he didn't get too upset with Elvis. He said he had a gimmick, and it was working for him. We would swoon all night with Elvis. He was rock-and-roll, and so were we. We are the generation that started rock-and-roll. The coal camp kids could take some credit for that. We all contributed to it. Rock-and-roll music went something like this: "You ain't nothing but a hound dog," or "Love me tender love me true." See, Elvis with all his swinging hips never used the kind of lyrics that you hear in songs today.

Chapter Fifteen

UNCLE ALEX AND AUNT JULIA AND BEVERLY MEETS RONNIE

I want to tell you about my aunt Julie and uncle Alex. They lived in the coal camp. Their children played with me all the time. Being that we were cousins, we did fight a little. Geraldine taught me how to smoke. I didn't know about inhaling the smoke. Norma was real pretty and acted grown up. She wore her make up even if she wasn't going anywhere. What a waste. My aunt and uncle both played the guitar and sang real pretty. I visited their house a lot. I loved to sing and play the guitar right along with them. Uncle Alex directed the choir at the Baptist church where I went to worship every Sunday morning. They read music and I didn't, so my uncle wanted to teach me; I told him no. I said I'll just use my God-given talent. And I have all my life.

The thing I loved most about Cinco was the people, just good, down-to-earth folks that loved God and their country. I also loved the holler above Patsy Mullins' house. It was the last house in the holler. I had lived there until I turned four. The water was ice cold year round in the creek that ran by their house. Patsy and I used to take a bar of soap and a washcloth and bathe in the creek. We were coal camp kids. Most of us lived in a four-room house that had a path not a bath. We kept warm mostly from the coal-burning fireplace we had. We all smelled like coal, but we didn't care. We also had number two washtubs. They were used for laundry and taking a bath on Saturday.

When Judy Bartley came to our house, Daddy would play the guitar and tell her to sing him a song. Judy had a real good voice, and Daddy loved to hear her sing. I'd love to hear her sing again too. I would request "How Much is that Doggie in the Window?" I know she knows that song.

Another friend of mine was Beverly Elswick. She moved into the last house in the holler when she was about thirteen; the same house I had lived in until I was four. Beverly was so much fun to hang around with. We would climb on the church bus and go to Charleston to the Pentecostal church where all the good music was at. We also liked the boys that rode the bus with us. Daddy put a stop to me going after he learned I was not going to a Baptist church. We made endless trips up and down Slate Lick Hollow. We rode the school bus to school and home every day. We took long walks together. We were both coal camp kids.

Beverly was born in the Putney coal camp. She lived there until she was about thirteen, and then she moved to Cinco. My mom had a little restaurant right above Midway Junior High School. A lot of the school kids ate lunch there. It was called Suzy Q's. They sold hot dogs, chips, and soft drinks. It had a juke box and pinball machines and attracted a lot of young people. One night, I talked Beverly into going with me to Suzy Q's. I told her that a lot of good-looking boys hung out there and she might meet someone. Well she did. That's the night I introduced Beverly to her husband-to-be.

The next story I am going to tell you is a true love story. The first night Beverly was there, a good-looking guy came to the counter and got a soft drink. He was drinking RC cola. He took it back to the pinball machine he was playing. After that, he came back several more times to get a drink. Beverly finally asked him what he was doing with all that pop. He said he was drinking it and asked her if she wanted one. She said no. Then after thinking about it for awhile, and seeing that he was so good looking, she went back to the pinball machine and told him that she would take that pop now. The young man was named Ronnie Marshall.

After that night, he went to see her at school every day. For him it was love at first sight. He asked Beverly how old she was, and she said she was fifteen. She lied; she was only fourteen. Beverly and I spent a lot of time analyzing this relationship she was in. We were always laughing at poor Ronnie. He never took us seriously. Then one day he told her he was coming to her house to see her. She told him he had better not; her mom would run him off. Ronnie just flashed her that winning smile and said he would see her there. I thought he was kidding her until one day she came running into my house and said, "Margie, Ronnie is up to my house. Mom is going to kill me." At age fourteen, her mom wouldn't let her date yet. Ronnie thought she was fifteen. Man what a sin she was stuck in. I told her I would go home with her. I didn't think her mom would kill her if I was with her.

When we got there, Ronnie and Beverly's mom were enjoying a good conversation together. See he was a nice guy with good manners and a winning personality. There was nothing not to like about Ronnie. Her mother actually liked him very much. So, the courtship was on. Over the next few years, they were inseparable. On her seventeenth birthday, he gave her a ring and asked her to marry him. They were married about a month later. She skipped school to go get a blood test and apply for a marriage license. She tricked her daddy into signing her marriage license. Back in the day, you had to have a parent's permission to marry if you were under eighteen.

Beverly's daddy didn't read, so she and Ronnie had Ray Keller (the local notary) to come to the house and let her dad put his "X" on the paper so he could notarize it. Beverly knew her mom wouldn't sign her papers, but since her dad didn't read, he wouldn't know what he was signing. Beverly was determined to marry the man she loved. She told her dad after he had put his "X" on the paper that he had just given her to Ronnie. That was okay with her.

Ronnie was from Reed. He worked for Amherst Coal Company. He took Beverly to his mom and dad's house. That's where they were married. They spent their wedding night in the house with Ronnie's family. Beverly sat in a chair all night. She was afraid to go to bed. There were too many people in the house with them. When Ronnie asked her if she was coming to bed, she said no. (Imagine that. Beverly, it's your honeymoon!) He told her she would get cold sitting in that chair. Finally, later in the night, it got so cold she had to climb into bed. A month later they got their own house and went to housekeeping.

When I called Beverly to tell her about the book, she sounded so sad it was shocking. She always had such a bubbly personality. She told me about Ronnie's death. Although he had been dead for three years, her heart was still so broken that she could barely go on. He had died unexpectedly in his sleep, and the shock almost killed her. Then I knew why she was so sad. Ronnie and Beverly were married for forty nine and a half years. Those years had been filled with joy but tempered with sadness. Their first child, Opal Louise, was stillborn. It was a very sad time for them. Then they had Mary Ann and Don, and their hearts were filled with joy. They adopted a son named John when he was twenty-one days old. Their joy was complete. Beverly said about six months after she lost Ronnie to a heart attack, she lost her son John to a brain tumor. That was almost more heartache than she could take. She told me that Ronnie was her life. She loved him from the first day she met him, until the day he died, and she still loves him. I knew I must pray for her and have others to pray for her. We were coal camp kids, and the bonds that held us together are never broken. She is as precious to me now as she had been when we were kids living in Cinco. I know her story is sad, but this book wouldn't be complete without Beverly in it. Her life with Ronnie was very happy. He was a good husband, father, and grandfather. I am so glad that I had the privilege of introducing that young girl and boy all those years ago. Beverly knows they will meet again one day in their heavenly home. What a day that will be. What a love story they have given us all.

Chapter Sixteen

FRIENDS LIKE BONNIE, EMMA, AND STEVE

I met Bonnie Stone at Midway Junior High school where we both attended. She was from the Point Lick coal camp. We were walking around the school; she was headed in one direction and I was going in the other. We looked at each other, smiled, and we both said hi. From then on, we were friends in the making. Although we had never laid eyes on each other before that day, it seemed as though we should know each other. Years later when we officially become friends, we talked about the strangeness of that day. I guess it could be the coal camp connection at work again.

When Bonnie was little she used to say she wanted to marry a preacher so he could keep her in line. Well, God heard her and sent her one of the good old boys, a real red neck from the mouth of Point Lick Holler. He wasn't even a Christian. A few years later, she finally got him to go to church with her; and wouldn't you know, he got saved. Soon after that, God called him to preach. "God will answer your prayers," she said, "so you better be careful what you ask for."

One night some years later, I walked into a church. There sat Bonnie, all grown up. Her husband was the pastor of the church. He was preaching "hell hot and heaven sweet." He knows the word of God and how to preach it. I don't know if he can keep her in line or not, but he can take the word of God and tear the hide off of all of us, her included. She has a wonderful Christian husband and he pastors the Rensford Independent Missionary Baptist Church located at Point Lick. His name is George Edward Jarrett. We call him Ed. Some still call him Red because he used to have red hair. Just think, little Bonnie Stone is the wife of a preacher man. They have been married more than forty years. How ironic is that?

Anyway the next day Bonnie called me; we talked for hours, and that restarted a friendship that will never end. Over thirty years ago, she gave me a copy of *The Open Bible* that I had been wanting for a while. I still carry that same Bible today. She is the best friend I ever had, next to Jesus. We plan on being best friends even in heaven. See we are both coal camp kids. Those bonds last forever.

Bonnie and her friends kept the fun going at the Point Lick coal camp. That's where she lived right next door to Preston Powers, that lucky girl. She had a friend named Freda. Now Freda's mom and dad had a hog which they kept in a pen. Adjoining the pen was a house for the hog to go into on hot days. One day as Bonnie and her friends, Linda and Barbara, were walking by Freda's house, (Freda wasn't home) they thought of how much fun it would be to shut the hog out of its house. So, they did. They put boards across the door. The hog didn't appreciate being blocked out of his house, so he charged the door. Now Bonnie was on top of the railing that went around the hog pen. The railing somehow broke. She fell and landed on the back of the hog. Don't you know she rode that hog until it literally scraped her off its back and threw her into his pen? She wallowed around in that filthy hog pen for a while before she could crawl out. She was covered from head to toe with hog yuck. She had to go home and face her mother as dirty and smelly as a hog. Now that took nerve, but that's one thing that Bonnie had lots of, nerve, and a knack for getting into trouble.

When Bonnie skipped school with her rowdy friends, they would hide in the graveyard all day. She said there wasn't much to do in the graveyard, so they read the headstones. After sitting around for hours and reading those names over and over, they felt like they were sitting among friends. After a few visits, they knew the names of all their graveyard buddies. Bonnie reasoned, and rightly so, that at least the dead couldn't tell on her. No one would think to look for her there.

One more thing I must confess to Bonnie: I told her I didn't skip school, but I did fake an illness every now and then so I could sit in my room and play the guitar all day. That might qualify as skipping. For the life of me, I don't understand how one little churchgoing girl could lie so much. That was a sin.

Bonnie was the baby in her family, and I was second oldest in mine. Her real name is Devonna, but we always called her Bonnie. She said her mother Dortha got her name from reading the newspaper in an outhouse. Now most people took a Sears and Roebuck catalog with them to the outhouse. Dortha was a little more sophisticated, and she was smart enough to know that newspaper made softer toilet paper than a catalog. Bonnie was in the sixth grade before she knew she had another name besides Bonnie. Her mother had given her the beautiful name of Devonna Lee and called her Bonnie all her life. (Now don't that make sense?) Bonnie said she sure didn't live up to her namesake. The article her mom was reading was about a girl named Devonna leaving for college. Bonnie didn't make it to college. (We all graduated from the school of hard knocks.)

I was named Marjorie by my parents, but the midwife couldn't spell my name, so years later, when I went to get a copy of my birth certificate, they found the error. Her attempt at Marjorie was illegible. Imagine my shock when down a few lines I saw that I was also registered as a male. Can you imagine what a mess this could have become if I had been dealing with a typical county bureaucrat? Luckily, the woman that was helping me had known me all my life. She told me she could make Margie out of what was written for my name. I told her that would be great, since that was what I had always gone by, and I never really liked Marjorie anyway. The addition of "fe" before the "male" was a much easier fix. Thinking back on this later, I wondered how I avoided the draft.

Being the baby in the family sometimes had its perks. Bonnie got to go trick-or-treating when she was real small. (I wasn't allowed to go until I started school.) She had a sister named Emma that would take her. One trick-or-treat night, Bonnie had a false face on that hindered her ability to see. Emma told her to take it off, but baby Bonnie wasn't about to part with her disguise. So she fell in the creek, head first. Not a clean creek either; it had coal dirt in it. That's where they washed the coal; so it was more like coal mud. Do you think that bothered Bonnie? No, not at all. What bothered Bonnie was that she was about to lose her candy. When Emma tried to pull her out of the creek, Bonnie fought her because she didn't want to lose her candy. I would have done the same thing. One night a year was all we had to get free candy, and we would keep that candy even if we drowned ourselves doing it. That's just the way it was when you were a coal camp kid.

If there was one thing all coal miners had, it was a belt. We called them bank belts. I don't know why. They were usually pretty wide, and they were made to keep your pants up and sometimes for clipping their carbide lights to. However, some coal miners had another use for their belts. Some used them to keep their kids in line. Mr. Stone (Bonnie's daddy) could pull that belt through the loops on his pants in a blink of an eye. It made a cracking sound that was your only warning that someone was going to get it. They all knew the sound of their daddy's belt coming off. One day Emma (Bonnie's sister) was fighting with her brother Steve, and her daddy got upset with them. After a while, he had had it with the two of them. As he ripped off his belt, Emma heard that sound and ran out the door. She pushed the door partially closed behind her. Well, her daddy was so mad at her that he ran into the door with that belt still in hand. When he hit the door, his pants fell down to the floor. Of course, Steve had run the other way. Bonnie saw it all, and she and her sister Mary started laughing because their daddy looked so funny standing there in his boxer shorts and T-shirt. He had a belt in his hand and a scowl on his face. She said he turned on them, and they had to run. Their Daddy pulled up his pants and gave chase. Emma ran as fast as she could to the tower where the mines kept all their water pumps and such. She didn't stop at the first level. She climbed all the way to the top of the tower. When her dad told her to come down, she said "No!" He said, "You'll have to come down sometime, Emma." She said, "And you will have to go to work sometime, Daddy." So she stayed in the tower until her daddy went to work that night. It was a very hot day and she like to burn up. It was a gutsy move, but Emma was a gutsy girl. She had stood up for her rights. By the next day, her dad wasn't mad at her anymore. She had escaped the wrath of her daddy's belt. Smart girl! (How high can you climb, Emma? Where did you go, Steve?)

Emma must have been her daddy's nightmare without even meaning to be. See in the coal camp, we all had linoleum on our living room floors. It didn't cover the whole floor, so we painted the wood that surrounded the linoleum. Now if you were at courting age, you kept them waxed until they shined, and then you lay down throw rugs to protect the wax. It also made the room look prettier. Now Emma had waxed the floor real good one day and put all the clean throw rugs in place. It was that same day that Steve acted up enough to get their daddy's belt in action. As their dad took off his belt real fast, Steve heard it crack and tried to run. Their dad took off after him, across Emma's newly waxed floor. Now Steve's daddy thought he was going to get away, so he kicked at him. He was determined to stop Steve somehow. However, just about the time he kicked one foot up in the air, the other was on the throw rug, and it started sliding with their daddy on it. Both his feet flew up into the air. He hit the floor with a loud bang. Can you imagine the frustration their dad felt? Bonnie said her daddy stayed on his back more than his feet trying to control the six kids that God had given him. Emma was a mixed bag that day. She was a hero to Steve and a menace to dad. (Go Emma, Go Emma) I guess Steve dodged the belt again.

Did you notice that every time Emma got into trouble, Steve always played a major role in it? It was just like Roy and me. I've said it once, and I'll say it again; little brothers are the enemy.

Steve was ornery, but little Bonnie, the baby, could be vengeful. There was a time when Dortha (Bonnie's mother) had gifts for Steve and Bonnie. She had two teddy bears and a doll. That morning as Dortha prepared to give the kids their presents, Connie, a cousin who never visited them, dropped by. Well, Dortha, being the good aunt, decided to give Connie a gift too. The problem was this: Dortha in her goodness mistakenly gave Connie the brown and yellow bear that Bonnie wanted. Steve chose the black and white bear. Well the only thing left was the doll. Bonnie had to take the doll. She was about five years old, and the baby of the family, and she thought that she should have gotten first choice. So for the next few days Bonnie was fuming. She was so angry: she couldn't believe that Connie had taken her bear. Her mother knew she didn't like dolls. How often did she get a present when it wasn't even Christmas? These were a few of the angry thoughts going through her little head.

So one morning Bonnie's mommy set up her washtubs and filled them with water. One was for bleaching and one was for rinsing. It was wash day and Bonnie usually hated washday. Soon the clothes were flying. Her mommy was washing, bleaching, rinsing, starching, and hanging her clothes out to dry. It just so happened that Steve had left his teddy bear lying in the kitchen. Now Bonnie, being full of anger because Cousin Connie had gotten her teddy bear, decided that Steve did not deserve one either. So, she took his teddy bear, put it in a huge tub of water, and held it under until it was good and soaked.

COAL CAMP KIDS | 85

So there, that's what happens when you ruffle the feathers of an angry little five year old. I do not know what Dortha did, but I'm sure Steve did some crying. That was revenge enough for Bonnie. At the time, she didn't understand that vengeance was the Lord's. However, the day Bonnie drowned Steve's bear, vengeance was hers. That's one time that Steve was purely innocent.

It was a well-known fact that coal camp girls could fight as well as any boy. We all had brothers. We didn't have any choice but to learn to defend ourselves from them. We got to where we could hold our own. One day as all the kids were going home on the school bus, a fight broke out between Hazel Powers and Frances Cox. Well the safety patrol on the bus was Ed Jarrett. Now Ed is the husband of Bonnie Stone-Jarrett. At the time, he was a school-age boy and the safety patrol. When the bus driver stopped at Ed's stop, the girls got off the bus to continue their fight. It was not their stop. They should have stayed on a few more stops before getting off. The driver, not knowing what else to do, told Ed it was his responsibility to stop the fight since he had a patrol badge. Well, Ed, feeling quite sophisticated, stepped into the middle of the fracas in an attempt to break up the fight. Wouldn't you know, those two coal camp girls turned on Ed and nearly beat him to death. When Ed finally crawled out from under those girls, he told that driver that if he wanted that fight stopped to stop it himself. Ed declared that he would never again get between two girls that wanted to fight. When girls wanted to fight, they would take on a boy as quick as they would take on another girl. This is especially true when they are raised in the coal camp. (Go Girls) After the girls whipped Ed, they kind of half laughed at him, got back on the bus, and went home. I don't think that Hazel or Frances are a part of Ed's congregation today. The enemy he fights now is Satan himself. If Hazel or Frances were in his church, he would probably still steer clear of them. (Go Preacher)

Chapter Seventeen

TATER-DIGGING TIME, NEIGHBORS, AND TRAINS

There was a woman who lived up the road from us. Her name was Rose, and she had a son named Charley. When we asked her when his birthday was, or how old he was, she would always say, "I don't know how old he is, but he was born in tater-digging time." I thought that was a good answer. I liked Rose. She wasn't educated, but she had a good heart and she loved her son above everything.

I remember when Charley was dating a woman named Mabel. They went to church every time the doors were open. They would walk back from church and sing all the way home.

It seems the children were not the only ones you could hear singing in the coal camp. Singing was good for your soul.

Joe Waughs lived above us with his wife. He was a big man. He had a horse and plow, and every spring he plowed up the ground for us to make a garden in. One evening as he headed home, I asked if

I could ride on his wagon. He said I could, and as soon as I got on, I got back off. I said, "I changed my mind, Joe." The smell of his horse made me sick. I don't know how Joe put up with that all day. Joe was always good to us kids; he looked out for us. Like one day, Ruth Ann White and I were playing together and the subject of cussing came up. We both knew some cuss words, but we were not allowed to say them. That day we decided we would cuss a little bit, express ourselves through the cuss words we knew. Even the really bad ones that we didn't know the meaning of. So as we walked down the road by Joe's house, we were cussing pretty good. He said, "Margie Pittman, just what do you think you are doing?" I told him, "We are just cussing up a storm, Joe." Man, I felt big. Well, Joe knew my dad pretty good, and he knew Dad did not allow me to talk like that. He said, "I wonder what Jesse Pittman would have to say about this?" Man, I saw my life passing before my eyes. I said, "Joe, please don't tell my daddy. I promise I will not ever do this again. Just don't tell my daddy." It wasn't that I was so afraid of my dad, but like my brother Larry, I did not want to disappoint him. He was too good to us for any of us to hurt him by disobeying him.

Living in a coal camp, you always had to deal with the trains that run up and down the tracks carrying coal from one place to another. Daddy always cautioned us not to get too close to the tracks. He said the train could suck us under the wheels. We respected that. Sometimes you would climb half way up the hill to get away from the tracks, but you never got so far you couldn't wave at the conductor and have him blow that whistle.

Now the Point Lick kids had a lot of fun on the railroad tracks. It seemed the Stone kids, Emma, Steve, Dickie, and Jimmy, along with the Horan kids, Richard, Carley, Merle, and Marvin, had a plan. They all waited until the train made its last trip for the day. When all the miners working the evening shift were in the mines, they would steal the pumper car. They would ride up and down the tracks from the head of Point Lick down to the end of Point Lick and back. I'm not sure, but I believe Jimmy Stone and Richard Horan drove the pumper car. They would have a ball riding that car for hours up and down the tracks. They always had it back before the shift ended. The miners never caught them. See they were coal camp kids just looking to have a little fun and do no harm.

Bonnie said her sister Emma was very kind to her. She would take her about anywhere she went. She must have thought the railroad tracks were too dangerous for the baby of the family. Bonnie, however, didn't appreciate them having all that fun without her. Sometimes being the baby is a heavy cross to bear.

My mother used to ride the train. She would take me with her sometimes. A day in town was great. A few dollars would buy a lot at the five-and-dime stores. S. S. Kresge's was a lot of fun for me. Woolworth's had a little snack bar. You could get something to eat and a fountain coke. I loved the taste of fountain coke and hot dogs.

Chapter Eighteen

SOMETIMES WE WERE SAD, HOT TODDIES, AND TEACHING SCHOOL

Things were not always good in the camp. Sometimes it was really sad. I remember a man called Jack, and I won't say his last name. He beat on his wife all the time. He would work all week and get drunk every weekend. That is when he beat on his wife. I never liked him, but I did like his wife. She was Betsy's sister. (Betsy and I did steal his chewing tobacco a few times.) I think her sister might have left him if she had anywhere to go. The worst part was she had three children growing up in this mess. I am so glad that battered women have somewhere to go for help today. I'm sure that there were many battered woman in the coal camps.

Everybody knew everybody in the coal camp. We were like a big family. We grew up in each others houses. The kids all played together. When we lost a friend in the camp, we all felt that loss deeply. I think all the coal camp kids felt that way. There is a bond that forms, and it is never broken. We knew all about each others business. It was just a different life, but it was a good life.

So many of the kids I grew up with have already left this earth. I miss them. Bonnie told me one day that there were only two of them left from her sixth-grade class. There is just her and a boy named Rudy. Sometimes I long to go back for just a few minutes to Cinco and see all the friends I had there. I would love to walk into the old company store one more time and get a free Pepsi-Cola from Lenny. When I close my eyes, I can still see Judy Bartley doing the jitterbug down at the Green Lizard.

Sometimes when I think of Mom and Dad, I imagine them looking very young. My brother Larry was always a girl-getter, so I had lots of friends whether I wanted them or not. They would come to the house on the pretense of seeing me, but they could not keep their eyes off of Larry. I guess we were poor, but we felt we were so rich. After my relatives left Cinco, our next-door neighbors were the Huffmans. There was Joyce, Jane, and Barbara. I used to go to the movies with Joyce when she was courting Charles. That is the way we did it back in the day. A girl never went out with a boy by herself. I would go so Joyce could go. Finally, they got married, had two children, and then got a divorce. I think he had a drinking problem. She was so beautiful; he should have treated her better. I never saw Joyce again, and the children were given up for adoption. As I said, there was some sadness to deal with too. I still miss her.

When I talked to Judy Bartley-Crews one day, I was amazed at how we still had similar memories of the people we grew up with. She and I go back to first grade, and we knew where everybody lived. You know she would say they lived at the corner house by the road that ran through the camp. I would say, "Yes, Joyce Case." We both remembered that she was beautiful and Larry had a crush on her. There were no secrets in the coal camp. Judy says I sound like my mother. She was close to mom, and I was to her mom. I took that as a compliment. As we grow older, we do become like our parents. That is not a bad thing.

Mom got real upset at a neighbor lady once. I will call her Mrs. M. When her husband would go out of town, she would ask Mom if I could spend the night at her house. She didn't have any children, and she would pay me fifty cents if I stayed with her. I was about ten I guess, and as soon as it got dark, she would lie down and ask me if I would fix her medicine for her. She gave me the directions on how to make it. First, you heated a little water and put some sugar in it, and then you measured out the medicine and stirred it all up real good. After she drank four or five of these medicines, she would go to sleep. One time when she wanted me to stay, for some reason Mom wanted me to stay at home. I told her I needed to go so I could fix her medicine for her. Mom asked what kind of medicine she needed me to fix. When I told her, she got very angry. I heard her tell my daddy I was making hot toddies for Mrs. M. I told them she was paying me fifty cents a night to do it. I think my dad got a little upset too. I did not know until I was much older that her medicine was really whiskey. What a real sin. They moved away right after that happened.

I forgot to tell you about my year of teaching school. You see I had two brothers and a sister in the little room. My sister Judy was afraid of everything, so she cried all day in class. Well, the little room teacher finally left and there was no one to teach the little kids. Mrs. Palmer was not about to take on both rooms, so I got elected to spend a lot of time in the little room. I remember my routine. I would walk into the room, get a paper towel, wet it good, and go wash Judy's face. She was always crying when I got there, but after I washed her face and talked to her for a minute, she would stop crying and enjoy school the rest of the day. My brothers would breathe a sigh of relief. They knew everything would be okay now. It was peaceful for the rest of the day. Judy wasn't afraid anymore, and we could even get some work done. It would have been a better job if I had been paid for teaching. Instead, it was more like babysitting. I still remember that little school house. It was one of my favorite places. We had two rooms, an outside toilet, and a pump from which we got water. After school let out, the playground served as a place for us to play. We never destroyed anything on that playground. We respected it too much.

One of my saddest memories is of a boy named Roger. I met him at the Green Lizard. He was sweet, but at a very young age, he drank too much alcohol. He used to walk me home from the Green Lizard sometimes. It was nothing serious; we were friends and sometimes we had a little crush on each other. I really couldn't let him be my boyfriend because he drank so much. One night it all ended when he was killed in a car crash. I still remember when they told me. I had already left the camp. However, I still cried for a week. He was so young; he should have stayed with us a lot longer. I still miss him.

I remember Betty Jo and June Kay Johnson. They grew up with us. For many years, we played and went to school together. One day they moved away. We sure missed them. They were good girls and fun to play with. They came back to visit a time or two. The last time they came, they stopped to see Judy Bartley; at least Betty Jo did. Judy asked her where June Kay was. They always came together. Betty had to give Judy the bad news. She had buried June Kay that day. I could have cried when Judy told me about that. Our friendships did not end when someone moved away. They live on in our hearts.

Chapter Nineteen

PLAYING KISSING GAMES AND THE CLOSING OF CINCO MINES

In my life, I had one birthday party. It was for my thirteenth birthday. A woman I babysat for gave me a wonderful party. Loraine (the lady I babysat for) baked me a big birthday cake with chocolate icing. She made bologna salad sandwiches and we had chips. By today's standards, that would not be a great party; well, I am here to tell you that we played kissing games until our lips nearly fell off. That takes a lot of kissing. My party, like all others in that day, had a little troublemaker. I hate to tell on him; his name was Jimmy, and if you were there, you know his last name. He went out on the front porch, took the fuse plug out of the fuse box, and shut the power off. I don't know exactly what he had in mind, but Loraine said if it wasn't back on by the count of three, the party would be over. He couldn't turn it on fast enough. We would all have killed him if he had broken up our party. Some of us had never played a kissing game before, and we were liking it. He said he was sorry, and I believed him. We were coal camp kids just trying to grow up.

I'm afraid that kids today don't know how to have the fun that we did. We were not bad kids, but we could get a little mean sometimes. We never damaged anybody's property. We did not disrespect our elders. We minded what our parents said, most of the time, or got into trouble. We never talked back to our teachers. If we had, they would have used a paddle on us for sure, and then we would have gotten another spanking from out parents. Children were taught morals in the coal camp. We loved God and would never make a mockery of his name. I would not trade my childhood for that of a rich kid. We were happy kids, and we were good kids.

I left the camp when I was sixteen, but my memories of growing up there are embedded in the Cinco coal camp. Today we still like to reminisce about our childhood in the coal camp. Those of us who are still living are friends to this day.

One thing our parents never had to deal with was obese children. We got up early, ate our breakfast, and then went outside to play. We climbed the hills, swam in the creek, and played in playhouses made with rocks and tin cans. We played games with each other such as jump rope, hopscotch, hide-and-seek, tag, and red rover. Daddy always had a vegetable garden. A saltshaker was about all I needed to have a good meal in the garden. Tomatoes, potatoes, and cucumbers from the garden and apples straight from the tree served us very well. They didn't need any cooking. They were good just the way they were. I learned in later years they were actually better for you raw than cooked. Imagine that.

Our supper most evenings consisted of pinto beans and fried potatoes, corn bread and green onions out of the garden. Mom would add to that corn on the cob, sliced tomatoes, and cucumbers. We ate good. Sunday was chicken day. Dad would kill a couple of hens right out of our yard, and Mom would bake a cake from scratch. No one ever got turned away from our table. The kids who played with us were as welcome as the aunts and uncles who showed up on Sunday.

After we played all day, we were ready to go to bed at night. We didn't sit in front of the TV all day, and we had no video games to play. All we had was each other and our imaginations to entertain us. I can tell you that was all we needed. We were happy, healthy God-fearing children. Kids today could learn a lot from coal camp kids. They could especially learn about honoring their parents, teachers, and elders.

One day Dad came home with sad news. The Cinco mines were closing down. He would have to find another job. He applied for a job in a union mines, and he was hired. He made a lot more money and didn't have to work nearly as hard. That mines was more modern. We stayed on at Cinco. It was home to us. The union mines didn't require workers to live in their houses. As I said, I didn't leave Cinco until I was sixteen. Dad worked in the union mines for eight years. When he had a heart attack, he had to leave the mines for good. The family moved to Daddy's home place. The house he grew up in had burned down, and Dad was left ten acres. When he could not work in the mines anymore, he built a house there. That is where he lived until he died. He was only fifty-four. We missed him so much at times, it was unbearable. He was a wonderful father.

Mom went to be with Jesus at the age of eighty-three. I am so thankful that God let us keep her as long as He did. A few years later, Judy left us for her home with Jesus. She is reunited with Mom and Dad forever. One by one, we will all join them in God's sweet heaven. I have been left to take care of my brothers. See somebody has to keep them in line. I've been trying to do that all my life. I have done a pretty good job.

The day Judy was born was the happiest day of my young life. The day she died was the saddest. I will always miss her. Judy was married to Ronnie. They had two children, Paul and Annette. They also have grandchildren. Ronnie is a wonderful grandfather. Judy loved her children and grandchildren with all her heart. She is waiting for them in heaven.

Roy and his wife Wanda had one child together, A boy named Shawn. But they have raised many other kids. I am so proud of Roy and Wanda. They have adopted five more children to love and raise. See Roy, with all his fun-loving ways, had the biggest heart of all. He and Wanda have both been saved. The children are taught that they are loved and that Jesus is their dearest friend. We all love the children and are blessed to have them in our family. Roy and Wanda are also grandparents.

Larry married Josephine and they had four children: Kenny, Rusty, Bobby, and Leona. Josephine followed Mom straight into heaven. She died one year after Mom. Judy left two years after Josephine. They always hung around together on earth. Now they will spend eternity together in heaven. Larry has a whole bunch of grand-kids. They think their Pa-Pa is the coolest. He always was.

Raymond married a girl named Judy. They have two children living and a little boy that didn't make it in this world, but they will all be together in heaven. Their children's names are Jessica, Ray, and Derrick. Raymond and Judy have beautiful grandchildren. They are wonderful grandparents. God bless the little children.

As I told you earlier, David married Peggy. They have two children, Missy and Jamie. Both girls have given them grandchildren. David, the good brother/tattle teller/smart boy, is a wonderful husband, father, grandfather, and as always, the "baby." He has always been a ray of sunshine from God. God bless the family.

My children are my heart. There is Sandy, Lori, Barbara, Michelle, and Junior. I have twelve grandchildren. God knew I needed a lot of kids in my life. I met and married a wonderful man about nineteen years ago. Bert is the love of my life. I am blessed.

The children I told you about are all grown now with children and grandchildren. Some of them have gone on to be with the Lord. Many of them have taken this journey with me down memory lane.

Life was simpler then and so much better. Our coal camp days are behind us, but they will never be forgotten.

As Loretta Lynn said, "A lot of things have changed since way back then." Bonnie and I went to visit Cinco coal camp last summer. The houses have been torn down and replaced with mobile homes. The old store has been torn down, and the beer joint is boarded up. There is a new Baptist church and the old Holiness church is still standing tall and proud. I went to the holler where I grew up. Our house has been torn down. It has been replaced by a mobile home. The creek is still there, and I wonder how many of Judy's panties are still stuck under a rock somewhere in there.

You cannot drive up the holler, it is all grown up, and the road is gone now. Bonnie and I went as far as we dared. We couldn't chance tearing the car up. For a few minutes, we were kids again on an adventure. It took us a few tries before we got her car turned around. We decided we had turned on a dime. (That is definitely coal camp language.) We then drove back out of the holler. It made me sad to leave. Somewhere deep inside, Cinco is still my home, if only in my memories. I will always be a coal miner's daughter, and I will always be a coal camp kid.

THE END

I want to acknowledge the ones who have gone on to meet God.

Cinco coal camp loved ones already gone:

Claude Bartley, Ruby and Reve Bartley, Jerry Bartley, Rose Bartley, Charles Bartley. Junior Adkins (Ruby's Brother) Judy Pittman-Quantrill, Geraldine Pittman-Decker, Kathy Pittman-Middleton, Richard Pittman, Alex and Julie Pittman, Jesse and Jane Pittman, Harold and Patsy Pittman, Johnny Pittman, Sidney and Thelma Pittman, Effie Pittman, Jenny Pittman-Newman, John and Ida Ulbrich, Norma Ulbrich, Kenny Ulbrich, Irene Mack, Carlos Elkins, Tracy Elkins, Opal Elkins, Linda Elkins, Jewel Cottrell, Lowell Craddock, Jerry Hicks, Nancy Lowry, Wayne Lowry, Mac and Ollie King, Sylvia Barnes, Ira and Dovie Pennington, Bill White, June Kay Johnson.
I'm sure there were others; I want to say to all their loved ones that they are missed.

Point Lick coal camp loved ones already gone:

Larry Lucas, John Lucas, Arvin Lucas, Gene Page, Edna Page, Carley Horn, Merle Horn, Lois Horn, John Douglas, Buddy Kozen, Gary Kozen, Sammy Brown, Phil Flowers, Glen Pruney, Barbara Adkins, Clarence Mooney, Ellen Powers, Robert and Dortha Stone, Clarence Adkins, Melvin Blankenship, Janice Blankenship, Drema Blankenship, Pat Mullins, Freddie Welch, Herbert Welch.

I'm sure there are many others. All are sadly missed.

Special thanks to:

Judy Bartley Crews for information about Cinco coal camp;
Bonnie Stone Jarrett for information about Point Lick coal camp;
Pauline Morris-Tucker for information on the boys of Cinco;
Larry, David, Roy, and Raymond Pittman for sharing their stories;
Bert Jernigan for all the hard work he did getting this book ready to print;
Sandy Debolt for her support in my effort;
Laura McGinn for her work editing this book;
Aurthor House Publishing for being so good to work with;

All the wonderful people who make Campbells Creek, West Virginia the best place in the world;

Our parents who let us grow up as coal camp kids; and

God, who is always there for the coal camp kids.